SALES FUNN▔

How To Rhythmicall▁   ▁▁ʊomers
And Unlock The Missing   ▁▁n In Your Business

www.salesfunnelsmadesimple.co.uk

Published by
Beach Group Publishing

On behalf of Sales Funnels Made Simple

Brands of Beach Group Ltd
153 Tilehouse Green Lane
Knowle
Solihull
B93 9EB

978 - 1 - 326 – 87979 - 2

www.salesfunnelsmadesimple.co.uk

ABOUT THE AUTHOR

Born in Watford in 1966, Barry Allaway has built up an extensive and impressive business portfolio during the course of his thirty five year career. With the last three decades spent in consumer magazine publishing, sales, marketing and logistics the last 15 years at Director/Board level.

Barry has extensive knowledge and experience gained through a range of senior roles; most recently as Managing Director of a magazine wholesaler and prior to that as Client Circulation and International Operations Director for IPC Media's Circulation arm (Marketforce) part of Time Inc, and AOL Time Warner company.

Barry's vast experience in strategy, big picture thinking and sales and marketing strategies that drive customer/client acquisition and retention, making him a sought after mentor, Non Executive Director and business angel/partner in the UK and further afield.

Barry is married to Hazel, and has two sons, Callum and Eachan. Outside of his working schedule, Barry enjoys sport, and is an active member of his local business community, as well as being president of his local Rotary club.

ACKNOWLEDGEMENTS

First and foremost, I would like to thank my immediate family, Hazel, Callum and Eachan, for putting up with so many of my spare hours being dedicated to the creation of this book.

Thank you for your support, patience, and most of all, your constant belief in me.

I would also like to thank all of the people, without whom, this book wouldn't have been possible. To Georgina El Morshdy, my Editor in Chief and all things content based. Tim Cooper-Cocks for road testing the Sales Funnels Made Simple concept, and Karen Blake for the funnel drawings, and book layout and design. Your patience, assistance, guidance and honesty have helped to create a book and business model I am really proud of.

To all the Entrepreneur's Circle members, 4Networking, BNI, Bob Club, Chamber of Commerce and Institute of Directors contacts – thank you for your encouragement, support and feedback on the concepts I have shared with you.

Thank you to my parents, Carol and Alan Allaway, for always believing in me and providing me with the ambition and determination to turn my dreams into reality.

And finally, a big thank you to the late Jim Rohn, whose famous quote has enabled me to stick to my goals during the tough times … "If the sky's the limit, how come there are footprints on the moon?"

SALES FUNNELS MADE SIMPLE

How To Rhythmically Acquire Customers
And Unlock The Missing Cash In Your Business

CONTENTS

INTRODUCTION

I cut my teeth in sales funnels in an unusual way.

For the best part of 35 years, I worked in the publishing industry –11 years of which was spent working as the managing director for the UK's leading specialist distributor.

The magazine business has been established for over 200 years.

As a result, it's a very traditional industry. It's one of the reasons our sales approach was largely passive. We'd wait for the phone call from a potential customer rather than drumming up business for ourselves. It was clear this was a problem. After all, specialist retailers don't wake up in the morning thinking that magazines may provide them with the answer they seek! As a result, our passive approach was limiting our growth. And in a declining industry this was a big problem.

We realised that specialist retailers need to be 'educated' – to help them understand the benefits magazines could offer their shops.

And as content and online marketing opportunities grew, it was clear we had the ability to make a serious impact. Better yet the opportunities were there.

We already knew there were around 250,000 retailers.

And after doing some data analysis, we discovered there were 190,000 retailers (across a total of 27 sectors) that were suitable outlets for selling magazines, but didn't stock the product currently.

At the time, we only supplied around 4,000 shops – about 0.75% of the total.

It meant there was a clear opportunity for significant growth, but this wouldn't happen if we continued with our passive approach.

It became a catalyst...

We needed to take responsibility for creating opportunities, but considering the size of the potential pool, it was important to find a method that wasn't reliant on manpower alone.

Instead, we needed to implement scalable systems and processes designed to initiate conversations with retailers and persuade them that magazines would make a profitable addition to their product range.

We needed to:

- Identify those retailers and sectors which offered the most potential – so we could focus our efforts and maximise our return
- Share a subtly different message with each sector – whether that was pets, arts & crafts, cycling, or cooking
- Explain the multiple ways shops could benefit from selling magazines
- Focus on building relationships with retailers – because it can take time to nurture and persuade a shop to get started

So, after calculating how much we could afford to spend to acquire a customer, we went about building a sales funnel with the right assets and touchpoints to attract the right leads and close sales. To do this we:

- Created educational content at the front of the funnel
- Developed a no-brainer offer that reduced the risk and allowed retailers to sell magazines for free
- Sent regular emails, direct mail, and newsletters to nurture the relationships and follow-up
- Made outbound telesales calls to those prospects that looked the most promising

And the results...

For a number of years, we outperformed the market by up to 25%.

Thanks to our sales funnel, we were able to place specialist titles into retailer outlets that wouldn't otherwise have sold magazines. It meant we continued to grow when the rest of the industry went into decline.

What's more, we did this sales and marketing activity profitably, because a significant chunk was automated and repeatable. And because we could track our progress every step of the way we always had a handle on what worked and what didn't.

And perhaps best of all, once set up, the funnel ran automatically – day and night. It was the reason our telesales team always had new leads to follow up and our orders continued to grow.

But here's what's interesting.

The lessons we learnt and the results we generated in magazine publishing were repeatable in other industries too.

It's why we've been able to help many businesses avoid the dreaded feast or famine syndrome – with the help of sales funnels.

You see many businesses have yet to master the rhythmic acquisition of customers.

Instead their leads (and sales) come in an unpredictable fashion and that uncertainty leads to a lot of unnecessary stress and sleepless nights.

Maybe the same is true for you...

When things are going well, you feel in control. But when the work dries up [or if you have an unusually quiet month], then the doubt kicks in, stress takes over, and overwhelm is the new norm.

Now the root cause of this particular business disease is lack of consistency – and a sales funnel is the remedy that can fix this challenge permanently.

That's because the rhythmic acquisition of customers (a system whereby you use a sales funnel to capture high quality leads – and nurture them over time into a customer), allows you to free up your time, reduce the stress, and grow your business daily.

And as well as helping you make more sales, it's a system that can offer more security too – something that's often lacking in the world of SME businesses.

So if you're always chasing leads, get slowed down because you lack systems, and know you would benefit from a simple breakdown to help you get your first funnel set up, this book is for you.

This book is chock-full of practical steps and swipeable examples.

We're not going to bog you down with theory and leave you wondering how you can make any of this happen for yourself.

Instead, we're going to arm you with the information you need to build your very first sales funnel – so you can start rhythmically acquiring customers fast.

Sales funnels have been the lifeblood of all of my businesses and it's the core asset that's driving success for our clients across many different sectors, B2B (Business to Business), B2C (Business to Consumer) and even in the third sector (Charities and Not for Profits).

As a serial implementer I get itchy feet! I enjoy idea generation and testing out new ideas. But I can do that because I have proven sales funnels that take care of the lead generation for me – even when my focus is (temporarily) elsewhere.

I hope that after reading (and digesting this book) you can enjoy the same results for yourself.

Here's to your business success.

Barry Allaway

The Business Alchemist and founder of Sales Funnels Made Simple

August 2017

CHAPTER 1

WHAT IS A SALES FUNNEL?
[and why you need one.]

Customers are the lifeblood of your business.

Which means sales and marketing MUST take up a significant chunk of your energy and focus. After all, if you're not investing the time and creativity needed to find and keep clients, the leads could dry up and you'll struggle to hit your sales and growth targets.

The challenge is you have so many other priorities on your plate.

You may even find that you don't have enough time to focus on this essential business activity because you're swamped with all the day-to-day priorities.

But that's not all...

When you do make time, it can lead to frustrations. That's because not all leads and clients are created the same.

Have you ever found yourself investing hours in a particular lead that never went anywhere?

Alternatively, there were some clients who needed very little encouragement at all before they made their decision. They just knew your business was the right one for them.

The challenge is you never know which type of lead they'll be at the start of your relationship together.

But if you have too many of the first type of customer, and not enough of the second you're going to waste a lot of time (and get frustrated at your lack of results).

So here's the thing...

You want to avoid the panic and fear of insufficient work.

But at the same time, you want to leverage your time and minimise the amount of your attention that gets spent on leads that are never going to convert.

And that in a nutshell is why you need a sales funnel.

Let me explain...

A **sales funnel** allows you to *visualise, organise, and systemise* the process that attracts leads – and then nurtures them to become your customer.

It's a process that changes the way you approach your sales and marketing.

That's because instead of frantically putting out feelers when you're desperate for work or handling each sale differently, you can put together a standardised, repeatable process – much of which can be automated.

It's a proven way to attract the right audience and make more sales – even when you sleep! What's more, when you do find the right people, it's easier to close the deal too. That's because instead of jumping straight to the close, you can educate and nurture a prospect first, so they can make an informed decision – when they feel comfortable.

With a sales funnel you can make follow-up effortless.

This is important...

Nowadays buyers often buy on the 8th, 9th, or even the 10th touchpoint – sometimes it takes even longer. Despite this, many businesses give up after two or three tries and therefore leave a heap of missed opportunities.

And your clients benefit too. That's because before a prospect becomes a customer, thanks to your sales funnel they'll already be familiar with who you are, what you do, how you help, and why you're an expert worth considering. You see, a sales funnel isn't just about a sales conversation, it's also a nurturing and educational process too. With the help of your sales funnel, you can make it easy for a prospect to:

1. Read some of your best content

2. Book a call or a demonstration with you

3. Enrol in a free course or watch some of your online video content

Whatever works best for your positioning, your sales process, and your capacity.

There are many benefits to taking this approach.

Get your sales funnel right and not only can you maximise the likelihood of a lead becoming a customer, but you can also weed out the timewasters before they become an energy drain on you.

But that's not all...

When you take this systemised approach, you can make your process slick, seamless, and efficient.

You can even identify the stages that slow down a sale or turn people off altogether.

And perhaps most importantly, because there are sections of your sales funnel that you can automate, this is also a tool that can free up your time and boost your efficiency.

That's why your sales funnel can become a powerful sales and marketing system that can transform your business.

THEORY INTO PRACTICE

Is your sales and marketing process efficient?

Do you struggle with the feast or famine syndrome? Do you waste too much time on leads that never convert or attract people who aren't a good fit for your business?

1. Take 10 minutes now to map out how you currently manage your sales process.

2. Note down opportunities for improvement.

Quick Summary: Why your business needs a sales funnel

1. **SYSTEMISE**

   A sales funnel ensures your sales process is repeatable and scalable (rather than subtly different every time you get a new enquiry). This cuts out wasteful repetition and standardises the way your business operates. As a result you can close more deals (more easily) and embed the foundations needed to help your business to grow and scale.

2. **AUTOMATE**

   You can automate aspects of your sales funnel using a range of tech. This means you can set things up to just run, and run, and run. No additional thinking or time needed. This can save money too. That's because parts of the process that you may have done manually can now be set up once – to run again and again. What's more, because this process happens 24/7 (even when you're asleep), your business doesn't have to stop just because you've clocked off for the day or you're taking a holiday.

3. **SAVE TIME (AND MONEY)**

   With a systemised, automated sales funnel in your business, you'll have less ad hoc work to do and therefore more time to tackle the mountain of other pressing priorities on your plate. And because things happen quicker (even automated), it means the cost of finding and keeping customers reduces too, which is good news for your profits and bottom line. It also means you could free up more money to invest in your customer acquisition strategy.

4. **FOLLOW-UP**

   Most new customers don't buy the first time they meet you and most businesses give up on the sale far too quickly when a 'yes' isn't immediately forthcoming. A sales funnel makes ongoing follow-up a breeze, which in turn can ramp up your conversion rate (and therefore your sales).

5. **AVOID THE DREADED FEAST AND FAMINE**

   Say goodbye to the unpredictable peaks and troughs and cut out the stress of wondering where your next sale will come from. A sales funnel is an asset that will help you rhythmically and systematically acquire new leads (and convert them) day after day after day.

6. **ATTRACT THE BEST CUSTOMERS**

   A key benefit of a sales funnel that includes a CAPTURE element is it encourages people to express their interest to you. You don't always have to be chasing leads, you can draw them to you instead. If you can build a database of people who have expressed an interest, no longer are you working with stone cold leads. Instead you can start nurturing people who have already seen something they liked. It makes it much easier to close the sale.

7. **FOUNDATIONS FOR GROWTH**

   Without repeatable/duplicative systems, your business is always going to have its limits. But introduce systems and automated processes that work over and over and you'll have a platform from which you can scale and grow more easily (and cost-effectively).

8. **CLOSE MORE DEALS**

   With automation and a system in place, you're less likely to allow leads to fall through the cracks – especially at the times when you're busy. As a result you could find this process helps you to find more customers. And because of the follow-up steps that you'll also integrate, the improved relationships you'll have with customers also means that you're more likely to keep customers for longer too.

9. **CONSISTENCY AND PROFESSIONALISM**

   A good sales funnel will outline the most efficient and cost-effective method to find and keep more customers. As a result, you can feel confident that ALL new leads are dealt with in a consistent way, which will make your business come across as more professional as a result. It also means once you start to grow and need more staff, you'll find it easier to 'show them the ropes' because there will be a set methodology to follow and utilise.

10. **PROFITABLE RELATIONSHIPS AND A HIGHER LIFETIME VALUE**

    With a Sales Ladder embedded into your Sales Funnel, not only are you converting prospects into customers, but you're also laying the foundations to increase your average customer value effortlessly by making it more likely that customers won't only buy more, but again at higher price points too.

So now that we've explored the benefits of a sales funnel and why you need one in your business, let's turn our attention to the nuts and bolts.

It's time to figure out what a sales funnel actually looks like.

The structure of a sales funnel

First things first...

All sales funnels differ, because for the best results they must be tailored to the business in which they're embedded.

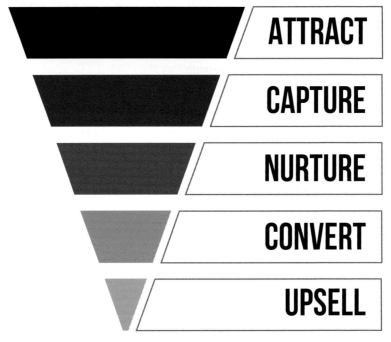

That said, there are some standardised stages which are present in virtually all funnels. So let's kick-start this section by exploring what these are first.

As you can see there are FIVE stages. These are:

1. Attract

2. Capture

3. Nurture

4. Convert

5. Upsell

Let's explore each of these in turn...

1. ATTRACT

The first job of your sales funnel is to encourage your perfect customer to raise their hands and express their interest in your business. The intention of this stage of the sales funnel is to ensure your offer appeals to a specific someone rather than a generic anyone. This helps to ensure that the leads you do attract are high-quality and a good fit for you.

You can attract leads in a variety of ways:

a. **Online** – someone reads an article or blog, engages with a social media post, or finds your business through Pay Per Click (i.e Google/Facebook) advertising

b. **Offline** – through direct mail, leaflets, newspaper ads, or telesales

c. **Face-to-face** – at your business premises, an exhibition, event, or when you're networking

d. **Through referrals** – someone else recommends your business and that contact gets in touch.

2. CAPTURE

Not everyone will be ready to buy the first time they encounter your business. That's why you need to capture contact details. Simply offer a free incentive that's enough to persuade a prospect to share an email address (and more contact details such as an address and phone number is ideal to aid follow-up) and then you have the information you need to stay in touch and start the follow-up process. We cover the CAPTURE stage in a lot more detail later in the book, but for now, here are some high-level suggestions, which can help you persuade prospects to hand over the details you need:

- Vouchers/offers
- Capture cards at events, exhibitions, or while networking
- Competitions and giveaways
- Slide deck circulation following a speaking gig
- Information freebies such as PDFs, e-books, and webinars

3. NURTURE

Some people will be ready to buy straight away, but more will require a bit more wooing than that! And with contact details collected, you have the data you need to build the relationship between you and your lead. This is about developing your 'know, like, trust' factor and it's a crucial nurturing step, which makes it more likely that people will feel certain it's the right decision to buy from you.

You'll likely need more than one touchpoint. In fact, most business give up on the follow-up far too soon. We recommend between 7-11 touchpoints, which can include any (or all) of the following:

a. **Content marketing** – when you create useful content to share with your list

b. **Email marketing** – where you continue the conversation in your prospect's inbox

c. **Social media** – where you share and initiate conversation on your social platforms

d. **Telemarketing** – where you speak directly with your prospects

e. **Demonstrations** – where you invite prospects to discover how to use your products

f. **Webinars** – where you share your expertise in a training-style format

g. **Consultations/meetings** – where you consult with a prospect to help them make their buying decision

h. **Facebook groups** – where you position yourself as an expert by offering advice, answering questions, or sharing resources in Facebook groups. Alternatively you could create your own (one of mine for example is called **Ninja Business Tools – www.ninjabusinesstools.co.uk**)

4. CONVERT

At the heart of the NURTURE stage of your sales funnel is follow-up. In other words, staying on the radar and introducing multiple 'touchpoints' – each time nudging a prospect closer to a buying decision. The number of contact points required will depend on what you're selling (and the readiness of your customer to buy). Your goal in the CONVERT stage is to change the relationship from prospect to customer and make your first sale – often by promoting a product at the lower end of your product range so they can check you out with minimal risk. Here are some ways you can secure this stage of the funnel:

- Kick-ass offers

- Outbound telesales calls

- Email and direct mail nurturing and pitching of your offer

5. UPSELL

A purchase doesn't necessarily mean your sales funnel has come to an end. Instead, that first sale is the trigger that can kick-start the next part of the process as you strengthen your relationship together and convince your customer to buy something else. You can do this by making additional offers and gradually inspiring your customer to want to invest further. This is called a **Sales Ladder** (as you can see in the diagram overleaf). Of course, not all clients will walk up the ladder rung by rung. Some customers will stay on the same rung forever, while some clients will jump right in at the top. The point is with the right process in place, you can cross-sell and upsell and entice people to keep moving – which in turn increases your lifetime customer value.

You can also DOWNSELL at this stage. If your first offer didn't convert, simply offer something else (that still adds value to your customer) and your sale funnel will work hard at increasing your sales and margins.

Here's how you can do this:

- Delivering on your promises, getting results, and building customer loyalty – so people want to buy something else

- Selling across your product range – so that your customers know what else there is they can buy

- Offering discounts – to persuade existing customers to invest in something else

In other words, not only can a sales funnel help you find a new customer, but it can be set up in such a way to increase the average lifetime value of each customer you do secure, by figuring out a strategy that makes them want to move up your Sales Ladder.

After all, I'm sure you have more than one product to sell, right?

To give you an example of this process in action, here's an example of what a Sales Ladder may look like for a typical expert business.

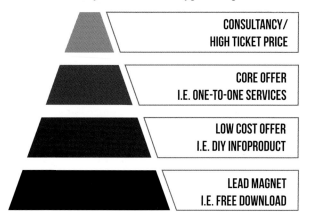

To show you how to put this into practice, here's what our Sales Ladder for our business looks like.

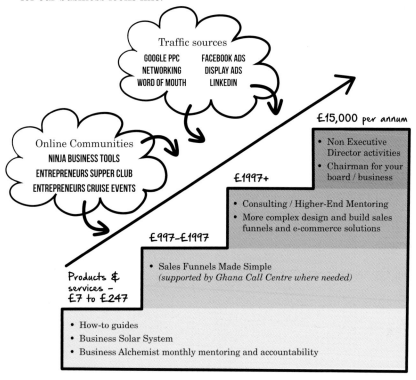

LEAD MAGNET

Our funnel is front loaded with free content. We've created something of value that will appeal to our target audience and that they can receive once contact details are shared.

DIY INFOPRODUCTS

We then start the nurture process and offer a low-priced, but high-value product designed to convert a lead into a paying customer. The bottom rungs of the ladder are filled with digital products and low-cost printed products – all designed to help our audience DIY their results. Note how these products help business owners implement the very results that our done-for-you services are designed for.

ONE-TO-ONE SERVICES

Moving to the next rung, customers can invest in one-to-one help and an entry level done-for-you service.

These services are designed for business that want more hand-holding or don't have the time, skills, or inclination to do things themselves. For example, we offer:

1. A monthly service where we'll help you build a simple sales funnel (www.salesfunnelsmadesimple.co.uk)

2. A monthly consultancy, advisory and accountability service where we'll help you put a monthly action plan in place to ensure your business is always moving forward (www.business-alchemist.co.uk)

CONSULTANCY

Move up the next rung and customers can secure more bespoke support and help from the team and me. This rung includes our bespoke funnel creation as well as 121 consulting with me through my Private Client Boutique (http://barry-allaway.com/private-client-boutique).

HIGHEST TICKET OFFER

At the top rung of the ladder is the opportunity to hire me to work as a non-executive director in your business. This service is the biggest commitment and also the highest priced offer. (www.barry-allaway.com/non-exec-director).

In summary, as clients move up the ladder, they pay more, but in return they enjoy a higher level of contact and support too.

But that's not all...

We've already revealed how a sales funnel can bring many practical benefits to your business – benefits such as time saving, efficiency, and an escape from the feast or famine syndrome.

But as the example above reveals, there's an even bigger prize to be won.

That's because if you build your sales funnel around a Sales Ladder, you don't have to worry about selling your high-ticket items from the off.

Instead, you can adopt the slow-burn approach and focus on building relationships instead. It's a strategy that can help you generate more profits in the long run by building more customer loyalty.

It's also a strategy that can remove your reliance on one particular product and instead add a layer of diversification into the mix.

And if you consider that on average, it's often found that 20% of your customers will buy the next level service [should you make it available to them!] you can see the potential for growth that's locked up in your business.

But how could this knowledge apply to your company?

What's in your Sales Ladder?

Before you keep reading, it's worth taking some time to think about the contents of your Sales Ladder. That's because this will form the foundations of your Sales Funnel (which we'll show you how to build in the next section.)

To do this, simply think about the various products that you offer and the various price points. As a general rule, the more value you add, the greater the price point the investment will be.

And if the concept of a Sales Ladder is new to you and you're unsure what best to include, remember we can cover this when you book your free consultancy call (details on how to access this as a buyer of this book can be found at the end of the book).

Do you have a Sales Ladder for your business?

If you do, take some time now to critique it and decide if you have the right products/services and price points at each rung.

If not, use the template below to start thinking about how you could increase your average customer value by organising your product range into a ladder designed to boost your sales and increase your profitability.

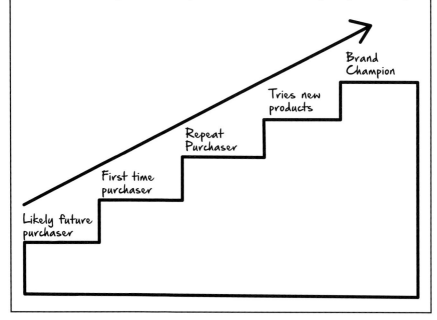

Moving on...

So now that we've outlined what a sales funnel is and why you need one for your business, let's start with the process of building yours.

We're going to start with the foundations – a piece of groundwork you must complete first, because otherwise all your work will be a waste of time.

I'm talking about **knowing who your customer is** – so you can be sure that all aspects of your sales funnel are appropriately targeted.

Let's turn our attention to your **customer avatar** and the theory of **Market, Message, Media**.

CHAPTER 2

SALES FUNNEL PREPARATION

In chapter 1 we talked about the structure of a sales funnel.

As a result, you should have a good idea of what your funnel could look like (and what products/services you want it to sell.)

But the structure of your sales funnel is just one part of the building process.

If you want to get great results, then you need to ensure your funnel will appeal to the people you most want to attract.

That means before you get building you first need to get thinking and strategizing.

In particular, you need to think about your **market, message,** and **media**.

Let me explain...

Market, Message, Media

Remember, your sales funnel isn't separate from your sales and marketing efforts, it's an integral part of this vital business function.

And because successful sales and marketing is dependent on the application of the **POWER TRIO** – aka, **Market, Message,** and **Media** (or the three Ms) – it means your sales funnel is too.

So let's kick-start your preparation work by exploring the three Ms in more detail – starting with some definitions of these key terms.

Market: The person/audience you wish your sales funnel to appeal to

Message: Your USP, your positioning, and your brand. What makes you special? Why should customers buy from you instead of your competitors?

Media: The methods through which you'll communicate your message through your sales funnel to your market. For example you may use:

- Leaflets, PPC or social media to ATTRACT
- Blog content to CAPTURE
- Direct mail to CONVERT etc.

So when designing your sales funnel, you need to consider all of the above – in the following order:

1. First identify your MARKET
2. Then determine your MESSAGE
3. Before picking your MEDIA distribution channel for each stage of your funnel

This order is non-negotiable!

Lots of business owners waste money because they jump straight to the what media decision.

But that approach is upside down. It's no good deciding how you'll send the message until you've figured out what that message is and who you want to send it to!

Let's do an exercise now to help you get this key information written down.

STEP 1 – KNOW YOUR MARKET AND CREATE A CUSTOMER AVATAR

Remember, one of the most powerful ways to ensure your sales funnel works is to get really clear on **WHO you want to attract and work with**.

That's why we're going to invest some time creating a customer avatar.

Specifically, this is a detailed understanding of your ideal customer in terms of their lifestyle, motivations, fears, desires, and goals (we've got a template coming up to help you with this).

This exercise is going to require some in-depth thought, so why not schedule in some undisturbed time to focus on it. You'll be glad you did! You see, once you know who you want to attract, knowing what to say to attract them becomes a whole lot easier (as you'll see shortly).

"But all my customers are all different?"

This is true! (And it's one of the excuses businesses make for not building out their avatar.)

But here's the thing...

This exercise isn't about packing all your customers into a tiny, rigid series of tick boxes and generic categories. In fact, depending on what you sell, you may find you have more than one customer avatar (and that's absolutely fine).

The key here is to **get comfortable with the fact that your business isn't for everyone** (unless you genuinely are a mass-market brand with a big advertising budget).

Whilst it's true that theoretically "everyone" could buy something from you, the reality is somewhat different.

In fact, if you look closely at your customer base, you'll find that there is a specific sort of person/people who you can (and do) best serve.

We're talking about the people who:

- Buy regularly

- Spend the most money

- Engage with you on social media

- Trust your expertise and value your experience

- Shout your praises to their friends and family, and

- Generally love what you do

These are your perfect customers – the people you want to fill your funnel with.

And once you figure out who they are then you can create a tight marketing message within your sales funnel that's going to give you much better results.

Here's why...

Imagine you were sitting in front of your perfect customer right now and had to sell them a specific service or a particular product, wouldn't you instinctively know what to say to close the deal?

You wouldn't feel tongue-tied or awkward. Instead, you'd be able to point out the benefits of the product, talk the language of your customer, and explain why it's a smart investment.

You wouldn't get lost in boring, irrelevant generalities, because you'd hone in on the specifics that sell.

And that's exactly what you need to replicate in your sales funnel... because when your target customer feels as though you're addressing them directly, they are far more likely to take notice of what you have to say.

This is why any sales funnel marketing that you create MUST begin by placing your target customer slap bang at the centre of your thought process.

So tell us, if you could wave a magic wand right now, what type of people would you most love to work with?

It's time to get thinking and complete your customer avatar.

Who's your perfect customer?

FIRST GET CLEAR ON THE BASICS...

Find out obvious stuff like:

GENDER	AGE
LIFESTYLE	
PROFESSION	
INCOME	

THEN PROBE DEEPER...

These "motivational" type questions enable you to understand at a more profound level, the type of person you want to attract and influence. See if you can find out:

WHAT THEY ASPIRE TO, DESIRE, AND WANT
THEIR FEARS, FRUSTRATIONS, AND CHALLENGES

WHAT KEEPS THEM UP AT NIGHT
WHAT THEY LIKE AND DISLIKE
WHAT CONVERSATIONS ARE HAPPENING IN THEIR HEADS AND AROUND THEIR KITCHEN TABLES
WHAT THEY READ
WHAT THEY WATCH ON TV (MORE STRICTLY AND X-FACTOR, OR PANORAMA AND QUESTION TIME?)
ON WHICH SOCIAL MEDIA CHANNELS THEY HANG OUT
HOW THEY RELAX
WHAT OBJECTIONS THEY HAVE TO BUYING
HOW THEY MAKE THEIR BUYING DECISIONS

Step 2 – Shape your MESSAGE with a big picture overview

Now that you know who you wish to attract to your business, the next step is to figure out what you need to say to make them come.

It's time to focus on your **message**... the **specific information** that you want your target customer to know. There are two levels to this:

At an **individual campaign level**, your message is likely to relate to a specific offer. In terms of your sales funnel, your message will focus on the next steps you want your audience to take based on the stage of the funnel they're at. So for example it could be:

- Download this free e-book because it will answer your questions

- Book a free consultation because it will help you create a strategy

- Buy this infoproduct because it will help you take action and get results

In comparison, at the **big picture level** your message is all about your positioning. In other words:

- Your Unique Selling Point (or USP)

- Your key differentiator... the "thing" that makes you different – the reason clients should "*know, like, and trust*" you

- The reasons why customers should spend their money with you instead of a competitor

You'll need both of these in your sales funnel.

The message for an individual campaign is usually fairly straightforward. Basically you need to:

1. Decide the action you want your audience to take

2. Promote the benefits of taking that action

3. Invite the reader to take action!

The positioning aspects are a little trickier, so to help, here are some probing questions to help you think about what makes your business unique – so you can ensure your audience understands why they should pick you and your business over your competitors.

WHY DO YOU DO WHAT YOU DO?

WHAT IS YOUR USP? WHAT MAKES YOUR BUSINESS 'SPECIAL'?

WHAT DO YOU DO/OFFER THAT YOUR COMPETITORS DON'T/CAN'T?

WHAT DO CUSTOMERS SAY THEY LOVE THE MOST ABOUT YOUR BUSINESS?

WHAT DO YOU WANT YOUR CUSTOMERS TO TELL OTHERS ABOUT YOUR BUSINESS AND YOUR PRODUCTS/ SERVICES?

Step 3 – Choose your MEDIA and decide how best to communicate your message at each stage of your sales funnel

The final step is to pick the right media to use within your sales funnel to communicate your message to your market.

There are countless ways to do this (and you can include a range in your sales funnel) – depending on which stage of the funnel you're working on (i.e. attract, convert, nurture, upsell etc.)

Here are some examples:

ATTRACT:
- Blog
- Social media (organic and paid)
- Leaflets
- YouTube videos
- Google ads
- Direct mail
- Networking/events
- Facebook adverts

NURTURE:
- Email
- Social media
- Retargeting
- Content marketing
- Video email

CONVERT:
- Email
- Website landing pages
- Your website
- Video sales letters
- Direct mail
- Lumpy mail (where you include 'grabbers' or small gifts to bulk out an envelope/parcel to build curiosity and increase the likelihood that your marketing will be opened)

WHAT'S NEXT?

Now before we get into the nitty-gritty of building your funnel, we need to focus in on the financials - so you can get clear on how much you can spend to kick-start your rhythmic customer acquisition strategy.

So let's turn our attention to the final preparation element, which is all about knowing your numbers.

In particular...

HOW MUCH CAN YOU AFFORD TO SPEND TO ATTRACT A PROSPECT AND CONVERT THEM INTO A CUSTOMER?

The short answer is a lot more than you think!

Here's why...

Besides all the psychology and sociology of marketing, if you want to get profitable results, there's also some cold, hard maths involved.

Now don't worry if maths isn't your strongest skill! This maths is easy and hugely worthwhile.

That's because I'm going to show you how to get clear on the amount of money you have to 'play' with to get your funnel working hard and attracting the right leads.

We're going to calculate your average **Customer Lifetime Value**...

In other words, how much is an average customer worth to you for the lifetime that they remain a client?

As you can imagine, this amount will be significantly higher than the amount of their first transaction with you.

Now most businesses don't think beyond the profits of that first sale and that's a mistake. You see, if you only focus on the profits from the first sale alone, you'll automatically dial down the amount of money you're prepared to invest to secure that customer.

In comparison, if you think about the bigger picture and how much a customer is worth longer term, you'll be more willing to invest more to attract and secure the best clients.

After all, if you can **outspend your competition** – you will win.

So how do you calculate how much an average customer is worth to you over their lifetime?

Let me show you this with the help of my Business Alchemy programme.

The monthly subscription to this service is **£99**.

Let's assume the average customer stays for 12 months. That means their lifetime value would be:

£99 x 12 = £1188

As you can see that's significantly higher than the first month's investment alone.

What's more, this amount could rise even further once a client has entered my Sales Ladder because I then have the opportunity to incentivise them to invest in other products and higher-level services (as do you).

This long-term approach means that (theoretically) I have more money to invest in finding the right customers.

Let's say I'm prepared to invest 15% of the amount that customers invest in my Business Alchemy service on marketing.

If I only consider the initial monthly payment, that leaves me with a **£15** marketing budget.

But if I base it on 15% of my customer lifetime value I have **£178.20** to invest.

Just imagine how much more I could do with that amount?

Remember, you shouldn't spend as little as possible to find and keep customers. Of course you want the numbers to work, but cutting corners with your marketing spend could suffocate your potential by preventing your message from reaching the right people.

Which makes the key question **how far are you willing to go?**

Could/would you spend £50, £100 even £200 to secure the perfect customer for your business?

As long as you can calculate the return you get from your marketing efforts, this lifetime value calculation gives you more flexibility over your customer acquisition strategy.

Note: The example above is for a consulting service with near 100% margins. If you sell a product or service that costs money to create and deliver, it's the net after-costs figure you should use to work this out.

THEORY INTO PRACTICE

1. What is your average customer lifetime value? Calculate it now.

2. How much are you willing to invest to find and keep the best customers?

3. With an increased budget available, what else could you do to stand out from the competition and close some new deals?

Moving on...

So now that the basics and preparation are covered, it's time to start building your very first sales funnel.

Let's lay the groundwork for the rhythmic acquisition of customers that runs on autopilot so you can make sales – even when you sleep.

CHAPTER 3
HOW TO BUILD YOUR OWN SIMPLE SALES FUNNEL

Introducing the Getting Started Funnel

At the heart of your sales funnel is the understanding that clients/customers won't always buy from you on their first encounter.

Of course this isn't always the case.

Sometimes the chemistry and timing is just right, but more often than not clients need time to warm to you – before they'll buy.

And that's what the Getting Started funnel enables.

It helps you to identify those people who may be interested in your services, and then stay in touch with them so you have time to build your know, like, trust factor.

It permits slow burn – which is what some businesses need. (And if you want fast burn, simply turn up the speed and intensity!)

This process allows potential clients to get to know more about you before they decide. It will also help them compare and contrast your offer with what else is available on the market.

As a result, when it IS the right time, your perfect customers are more likely to buy.

But how can you get to this point?

The onus has to be on **nurturing profitable relationships** and the way to do this is to:

- Show people what you can do *(know)*

- Share your personality *(like)*

- Prove you get the results you say you do *(trust)*

It's not enough to rely on gimmicks and never-ending promotions.

Instead you need to put in the work up front to prove that you are trustworthy and authoritative – and use your personality to attract the people who best resonate with you.

That's why your sales funnel must consist of numerous touchpoints – especially if you're selling something that's high value.

It means you've got to create and share the content that can help people make informed decisions.

And when someone raises their hands to show an interest, you need to be able to capitalise on that opportunity.

So, when someone shows an interest (even if they're not ready to buy right now), you still want to collect their details.

Then armed with an email address, postal address and/or phone number you can stay in touch with that person:

1. You can onboard them into your world (more on that shortly)
2. You can build your *know, like, trust* factor through content and conversations
3. You can make an introductory offer to turn a prospect into a customer
4. You can entice a customer to buy more
5. You can ask a customer to refer you to their friends

In short, build a list and you'll have your own audience that you have some control over. You don't have to wait for them to show up in your world again, you can take the conversation to them.

And that can make all the difference between a boost in sales this month – and a decline.

Too many businesses focus on the one-off promotions and short-term gains. Sure your strategy may be successful, but it's not sustainable because you'll be continuing the feast or famine cycle.

Instead you want to win AND (more importantly) KEEP customers – so they buy again and again.

And that's exactly what a sales funnel can help you achieve by focusing on **strategic relationship-building**.

If you can persuade someone to join your list, they become someone you can keep in the loop. Or, to put it another way, customers you can entice into buying more profitable goods.

And what's more, when customers are on your list, all is not lost if they miss out on a particular offer, low price or event. If you send regular updates, they'll catch the next one, so you give them the ability to take their time. You're always there for them, and what is better than that for a working relationship?

SO HOW DO YOU ADD PEOPLE TO YOUR LIST?

Here's the easiest way of all...

It's the GETTING STARTED funnel and here's what it looks like.

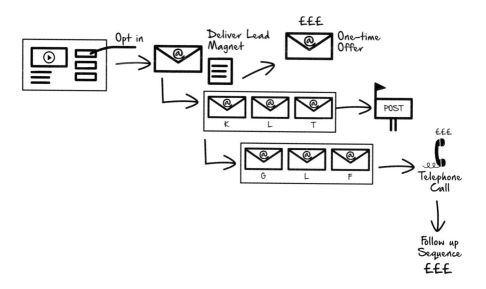

This funnel probably feels familiar – it's built on the examples we showed you in chapter 1 and as you can see it's driven by opt-ins. We have covered opt-in through to *know, like, trust* already. The *gain, logic, fear* (G-L-F) is covered later in the book.

Here are the five simple steps you need to follow to build yours.

STEP 1 — Create a **lead magnet** that your target customers find irresistible

STEP 2 — Build **capture pages** and capture those all-important contact details

STEP 3 — Drive **traffic** to your capture page

STEP 4 — **Deliver** your lead magnet and manage your new leads

STEP 5 — Email **onboarding** sequence – KLT, GLF

Step 1: Create a lead magnet that your target customers find irresistible

If you want to persuade people to join your list and share their contact details (so you can keep in touch), then you must give them an incentive.

This is your **lead magnet** and it's the asset that kick-starts your sales funnel.

In the past, you used to be able to just ask, but now people are more savvy.

They know what will happen if they share their details and they don't necessarily want to be swamped with emails and promotional bumf! There are other factors that make us reluctant too. Lack of time and constant demands on our attention make us pickier about whose list we get on. What's more, in a world where the border between private and public are increasingly blurred, many people are more protective over the information they give.

So unless you give your audience a good reason to opt-in, you'll struggle to collect those all-important details in the first place.

And that's why your lead magnet is crucial.

Let me explain...

The role of lead magnets in the sales process

A lead magnet is something of value (but free) that you offer a potential customer in order to obtain their contact details. Here are some examples that have worked well for some of our clients:

1. Mythbusters

2. 'How-to' guides and other valuable e-books

3. Access to a free course

4. A video series

5. An email course

6. Infographics

7. Quizzes

8. Competitions

9. Surveys

10. Webinars

11. Free gifts

12. Free consultations

13. A free trial period

14. A free sample/demonstration

15. A free site survey

16. Vouchers/coupons

17. A brochure/printed catalogue etc.

The purpose of a lead magnet is to offer a no-brainer incentive that encourages your potential customers to take the next step on their journey to becoming your customer.

As you can see from the list above, there are a few categories that work:

1. INFORMATION (INCLUDING E-BOOKS, INFOGRAPHICS, EMAIL COURSES, AND VIDEO SERIES)

Expert information is a proven method of driving sign-ups. One of the reasons this strategy works so well is because it aligns with the way people make buying decisions. For example, if you can provide content that answers some of your prospects' burning questions while showcasing your company's personality and proving that you're an expert, it can help you close the deal.

What's more, information is relatively easy and inexpensive to package up. And with design tools such as Canva, you can make your content look professional and eye-catching.

Here are some examples:

1. **Cleaning mythbusters** – to promote a company that offers commercial cleaning services

2. **A webinar** to get more done in 90 days than most businesses achieve in a year

3. **A checklist** to help you become an implementation master

2. TIME (INCLUDING CONSULTATIONS, DEMONSTRATIONS, AND ONSITE VISITS)

If you know you're more likely to close a sale after speaking with or meeting potential clients face-to-face, your lead magnet can be an offer of your time. For example:

1. **One alarm company** offers a free security review where they'll visit your home/business to help you understand your security risk and then present a solution

2. **One cleaning company** offers free demonstrations to help secure big contracts

3. **One copywriter** offers a free consultation to help map out your story so it becomes easier to share

3. FREEBIES (INCLUDING COMPETITION PRIZES, VOUCHERS, AND GIFTS ETC.)

People love freebies and offering something valuable for free can be enough of an incentive to persuade someone to part with their contact details. For example:

1. We have offered this book for free as an incentive to persuade people to join our list

2. When I worked in magazine distribution, we included vouchers for retailers in our free information pack that would give them free racking to the value of £750 – when they started selling magazines

3. We offer a free consultation worth £125 for business owners interested in getting started with a sales funnel

The key to a successful lead magnet is to offer something of perceived value that customers want and are willing to share their contact details to get.

THEORY INTO PRACTICE

What's the right lead magnet for you?

Take a few moments now to brainstorm your options under the three headings:

1. Information

2. Time

3. Freebies

And don't worry if you don't come up with the perfect solution the first time.

Every lead magnet you build is an asset that you can use to nurture relationships with your customers. The key is to test and experiment... and see what works for you.

N.B. There's more help coming up...

Here are some tips for creating three different types of information-based lead magnets.

1. MYTHBUSTERS

Are there myths attached to your industry that are leaving clients/customers uninformed and in the dark?

A mythbuster document not only addresses these myths (while positioning you as the one in the know), but can also prime the reader to change the way they think and feel about the service you offer.

You can also use this tool as a way to present your initial offer to people too.

Here are some top tips if you want to produce one of these:

1. **Start with a brainstorm**. Write down all the misconceptions and misunderstandings that happen in your industry. Once you've exhausted your own list you can add to it by:

   a. Asking your audience by email, on social media, by creating a survey, or when you're face to face

   b. Searching on Google

   c. Searching social media

2. **Next counter the myths**. Make a list of ideas that enable you to bust the myths you identified above.

3. **Shortlist**. Weed out the weak from the strong. Which myths listed above will resonate most and have the biggest impact on your audience... aim for six or seven.

4. **Next do your research**. Can you find statistics, facts, or case studies that back up your claims? Google is a great place to start because you can hunt down surveys, news stories, and in-depth reports to help you hang your hat on your claims.

5. **Presentation**. A mythbuster works best when it's a visual representation of your ideas. An infographic is a great way to present this. Aim to keep your text short and succinct and use graphics to pack a visual punch and tell the story.

6. **Call to action**. With the information part of your mythbuster complete, remember to include an invitation to take the next step so it becomes a tool that proactively drives your funnel.

2. CHECKLISTS

A quick and easy, but effective way to package up your expertise is with a checklist.

People are overwhelmed with information and advice, but nobody benefits from your ideas unless they get implementing. A checklist can help with that.

Is there a process you can help clients with that you can turn into a checklist? For example:

- The elements to create a leaflet that sells

- The nine habits of master implementers

- Seven checks to keep your office clean

You get the picture...

Simply list the points/steps you want your clients to follow (with a brief explanation) and add check boxes. Enlist the help of a designer to turn your ideas into something that's visually appealing and you're done!

You have a simple lead magnet that can add real value.

There are some unexpected bonuses with this form of lead magnet too:

- There's a chance a subscriber may print off copies of your checklist – so make sure you include contact details. If you have a physical presence in someone's life, you'll create a constant reminder of your existence.

- Checklists inspire action, which can lead to results. And if you've helped someone get a real outcome, what are the chances of them being excited to work with you?

3. DIAGRAMS

One of our most effective lead magnets is a series of sales funnel diagrams.

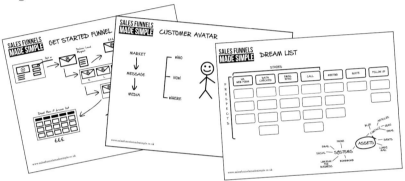

These diagrams are designed to show prospects a variety of funnels that could be embedded in their business. This lead magnet takes a visual approach which means they're easy to digest, yet still provide some key information.

And because the diagrams don't explain the How to Build, they're the perfect teaser for a free funnel consultation (which creates an opportunity for us to offer our monthly package).

But lead magnets are just a part of the sales funnel story.

Sure they kick-start the process by enticing the right people to raise their hands and indicate they are interested in what you have to offer. But to capitalise on the effort you went to create the freebie, you've got to find your audience and collect their contact details.

And that's why you need a capture page.

Let me explain…

Step 2: Create the opt-in process and capture those all-important contact details

Once you've created your lead magnet, you need to persuade your target customer to 'opt in' to receive it.

And to achieve this you need an opt-in form that's:

1. Built on a dedicated capture page

2. Embedded into your website

3. Appears as a pop up

Let's look at these three options in turn:

OPTION 1: CAPTURE PAGES

A capture page is simply a web page that's designed to encourage a visitor to share their contact details. Linked to your CRM or email marketing system, a capture page showcases your lead magnet, hosts an opt-in form, and provides the tools for you to build your list of prospective customers.

Remember, the sole purpose of your capture page is to encourage a page visitor to sign up to get your lead magnet. That is the ONE job of your capture page – nothing more. And that's why less is more. You don't have to sell the visitor on the virtues of your business. All you need to do is make the lead magnet so compelling, that the visitor won't leave until they've got whatever you're offering into their hands.

Here's an overview of the eight main elements of an effective capture page:

1. **HEADLINE:** Your headline is the most read part of the page. Its sole job is to hook in your web visitor and convince them to keep reading. Your headline should:

   - Appeal to the problem you're solving – e.g. 'Do you have trouble sleeping at night?'

   - Summarise its benefits – Finally, you can have the undisturbed sleep you crave

2. **BENEFITS:** Here's where you go into detail about how that need or problem is addressed by your lead magnet. In short, this is where you create a compelling case that persuades your visitor that they should opt in to your lead magnet. Remember, all your prospective customer wants to know is 'What's in it for me?" So make this abundantly clear. You can deliver this information through text or a video – even try both.

3. **CALL TO ACTION:** Once you've presented a compelling case that convinces a visitor to opt in, you need to tell them how to do it! This is your call to action. This shouldn't be complicated. The more specific and obvious you can get, the better. For example:

   • To get your free e-book, pop your details into the form below

4. **HERO IMAGE:** A visual image of your lead magnet can make it easier to 'sell' your freebie. It's easy to get bespoke images of your e-book cover, voucher etc. created:

   • Your **graphic designer** will be able to create something compelling

   • Try **Fiverr** or other gig-based sites

   • You can DIY with tools such as **Canva**

   • Alternatively, check out **Graphic Empire**, which contains a wide range of customisable graphics

5. **OPT-IN BOX:** This is the section of the capture page where you want customers to write their contact details. Your opt-in box (set up in your website or email system back end) should stand out from the rest of the page – for example, you could make it a different colour to the background.

   Your opt-in box should also contain the 'action button'. This is the button you want your readers to click to submit their contact details and kick-start the lead magnet delivery. Avoid action 'submit' (who wants to submit!) Instead, use your button to reaffirm what the visitor is opting in to get. For example:

   ### Yes! Please send my free report NOW!

   Another tip is to ensure the colour of the action button contrasts with the rest of your design. As a guide, oranges, greens, and yellows are effective call to action colours – especially if you're using black text on a white background, but don't take our word for it. The only way you'll know for sure is to test it.

6. **TESTIMONIALS:** We're a cynical bunch, so even if you write the world's most compelling copy, testimonials are still needed to give that all-important social proof that what you're saying about your lead magnet is true.

   It's for this reason you should always aim to include written or video testimonials from people who've benefited from your lead magnet – even better if the testimonial supports the claims you made in the benefits section.

7. **CREDIBILITY:** Not essential, but consider including a brief overview of you, your business, your success, who you've worked with, why you do what you do, and what you aim to achieve in the future. It helps to builds the 'know, like, trust' factor.

8. **LOGO:** It can pay to include your logo, but don't make this the main feature of your page – that's the job of your lead magnet.

There's a fine art to writing capture pages, so here are some dos and don'ts – to help you write pages that convert.

DO

- Concentrate on what your customer wants, NOT what you can give them. You're not 'selling' a lead magnet – you're promising to add value to their life in some small way.

- Use "you" as much as possible, and ease off using "we". It's a turn-off. Remember, all a customer wants to know is *what's in it for them*. Make sure you get your emphasis right.

- Be specific and concise. Your lead magnet should be an easy sell – not complicated. So don't waffle and over complicate your message. Remember, your message will be competing for space amongst plenty of other businesses. So don't lose out because you didn't hook in the right people.

- Constantly revisit. Just because you've created a lead magnet and associated capture page, don't assume your job is done. Things change. You learn more about what your customers want. You have fresh ideas or more knowledge. Always be looking for ways to improve your page and get more sign-ups – even if that means eventually you create something entirely new.

OPTION 2: EMBEDDED WEB FORMS

Capture pages are a brilliant way to showcase your lead magnet on a dedicated page – but it's not the only way to collect the contact details of prospective customers.

Many email marketing systems enable you to build opt-in forms, which you can embed onto your website using some code. If you're not web savvy, this sounds far more difficult than it actually is – just ask your web person, they'll get you set up in no time.

The advantage of an embedded web form is you can add an opt-in form to the bottom of a blog post or in your sidebar (for example). In short, you don't need to create a dedicated capture page to build your list – you can add opt-in functionality to existing content too.

OPTION 3: POP-UPS

Again, not difficult to do if you have the technical know-how to add this functionality to your website. There's a lot of debate as to the effectiveness (and annoyance) of pop-ups so this is something you really need to test to see if it works for you.

A pop-up is a small window that suddenly pops up in the foreground when a visitor is browsing your site. Opt-in forms promoting your lead magnet can be featured in the pop-up box and are therefore another good way to build your list. But beware… a pop-up can be annoying if it disturbs the flow of what your visitor is doing. In this way, pop-ups can be intrusive – because a visitor is forced to look at this message. In comparison, squeeze pages and embedded web forms are there to be discovered.

Pop-ups also include web chat and such technology.

What's the best option to use?

There is no right or wrong way to collect your customers' contact details. Arguably, the best solution is to use a combination of all three. Test it and discover which combination works right for you.

With the contact details secured, the next step is to deliver what you promised – that's why you need email marketing software.

Let's explore the detail…

Step 3: Drive traffic to your capture pages so you can build a list of perfect customers

With your lead magnet created and your capture page live, the next step is to ensure the right people see your offer.

It's time to get the eyes on your page by sending and attracting traffic. Let's explore some of the ways you can do this.

ORGANIC TRAFFIC

A relatively easy, long-term strategy for getting traffic to your website is by investing in your content marketing strategy and creating blogs.

Blogs have lots of benefits:

- Naturally incorporate key search terms and phrases and you can increase the likelihood that your business will show up in an organic search, which is great for your SEO (Search Engine Optimisation).

- The internet has changed how people make their buying decisions. Gone are the days when people relied on sales assistants alone to help them make their choice. Now people are more likely to self-educate before they get to that point. That's why smart businesses invest in content marketing.

- If you write useful blogs that answer questions, provide information, and add value, not only can you help people decide what product or service they need, but you can also increase the chances that it's YOU they'll decide to buy from.

A blog gives you a presence online and the opportunity to own your own publishing platform.

You can use your blog as a capture tool by including an opt-in box on each blog page. You can also promote your lead magnet in your blog content too. As a result, blogging can help build your list and boost the number of visitors to your website.

As with everything else, to get the best results from blogging you need to invest in creating content consistently and regularly. Whether that's weekly or monthly, get into the habit of publishing something at a specific frequency and you can keep seeing results.

Here are some blog ideas, which you could explore for your business:

1. **How To** posts

2. **List** posts

3. **Opinion posts:** Have a rant, express a controversial point of view, or talk about your niche from your unique perspective. This approach is great for initiating discussion, creating different camps, and differentiating yourself from the rest of the field

4. **Alternative posts:** Share a different approach to a common solution that your audience currently uses

5. **Current affairs posts:** Piggyback off a key event covered in mainstream news

6. **Subject-specific posts:** Comment on the hot trends, or put your spin on the big news, developments or events specific to your niche

7. **Mistakes posts:** Flag up the big mistakes that people make relating to an aspect of your specialist knowledge

8. **Lessons from posts:** Take inspiration from popular culture, TV shows, sporting events, or hit movies and create lessons that are relevant to your niche

9. **Predictions posts:** Show you're a thought leader by putting a stake in the ground and sharing your hot predictions for the future (with well-argued reasons of course)

10. **Reflective posts:** Look back on a period of time, an event, or a project and share your learnings, distinctions or insights

11. **Commentary posts:** Do a round-up of what other experts are saying, or write a commentary around someone else's thought piece

12. **Case study posts:** Put theory into practice and show how aspects of what you teach are working in other businesses

13. **Problem + Solution posts:** Exactly what it says! Present a common problem faced by your audience and then explain how to solve it

14. **Explanation posts:** Explain the reasons why a particular outcome occurs

15. **Ultimate guides:** As the title suggests. Write a comprehensive post that can be positioned as a "go-to" resource for a particular topic or subject

16. **Checklist posts:** Outline how to complete a particular task by taking the reader through a step-by-step checklist process

17. **Series:** Break down a complex or lengthy topic into a series of posts and link them together

18. **Signature system posts:** Describe your signature process/system/technique (or however else you present your unique spin on your topic to your audience)

19. **FAQ posts:** Answer the most common questions presented by your audience. This approach is great for proving you listen

20. **Definition posts:** Define key words and concepts relating to your niche and/or your system

21. **Revealing posts:** Let your guard down and share a heartfelt, truth that really lets your audience connect with you at a deep, emotional level. This can be a risky strategy, but revealing your vulnerabilities and your deepest thoughts can also warm people to you and boost your likeability

22. **Interview posts:** Interview your clients, other experts, or even have someone interview you and share the conversation on your blog

23. **Highlights/best of posts:** Great for summing up a topic or linking a number of blogs around a similar topic together

24. **Crowdsourced posts:** Ideal if you have a wider community around you and you wish you share other expert voices

25. **Diary posts:** Talk about events, review books and courses, or talk about other personal experiences that are relevant to your audience whilst sharing a little of your personal story

26. **Your product/service tips:** Help your customers get the most from their investment (and encourage others to sign up because they want a bit of the action too!)

27. **Set a challenge:** Invite your audience to join you for a challenge, which links into your products or services and which offers stacks of value and allows you to sell

28. **Capture posts:** Write a post that "sells" your lead magnet or tripwire and encourages your audience to take the next step along your sales journey

29. **Your first post:** Sometimes the first step is the hardest, so hand-hold your audience through doing something for the very first time.

SOCIAL MEDIA

Social media is an incredibly powerful tool which you can use to drive traffic into your sales funnel.

As you know, social media is perfect for two-way conversation. So instead of broadcasting your message, you have the opportunity to initiate and engage in conversations. As a result social media is the perfect way to showcase your expertise (so you can build your authority), but it's also a brilliant tactic for expressing your personality (and therefore building your likeability factor). Ensure you have a regular presence, keep your timeline relevant, and post regularly and you can generate profitable engagement that can drive your sales funnel.

Remember, you can't succeed on social media without a human approach. Sure there are automations and scheduling tools you can use to boost your efficiency and save time, but if you want real results you can't avoid rolling up your sleeves and spending some time online yourself.

You've got to share content, create your own, post pictures, share your successes, and tell stories. In other words, create a variety of content types to help build your online authority and become better known for who you can help – and how.

Here are a few strategies to explore:

- Post links to your blog posts to increase their visibility and collect shares

- Invest in paid advertising to send highly targeted traffic to your blog content and capture pages

- Join relevant social media groups and position yourself as an authority in your given field

- Create your own Facebook group and nurture relationships with your ideal customers in a designated community

- Include a link to your lead magnet in your social media bios

- Post a video or a record a Facebook livestream that talks about your lead magnet

PAID TRAFFIC

As you know, a huge percentage of purchases start with an online search. And while blog content can help boost your organic rankings, the only way you can guarantee yourself a top spot is by investing in paid Google ads.

The big benefit of this approach is people searching on Google are looking for something specific. It's not like social ads where you're trying to attract and distract from the sidelines. In the Search Engine Results (SERPS), customers are looking for you to solve their challenges and they want the answer now!

OTHER TYPES OF TRAFFIC

The above is not an exhaustive list of how you can send the right eyes to your content (so they can opt-in and kick-start your sales funnel). Here are some other tactics you can try:

1. **Be a guest** – for example, get interviewed on a Podcast, write a guest blog, or share your expertise in someone else's Facebook group

2. **Joint ventures** – find out who else has a list of your perfect customers and work out a deal whereby they promote you in return for some sort of reward

3. **YouTube** – this is a search engine in itself. Create some videos and get yourself found and you could boost your list easily

4. **Influencers** – build relationships with people who can promote you, recommend you, and refer people to you

In the past I have even experimented with bespoke **scratchcards**. It was a strategy that worked brilliantly for sectors such as restaurants. I also tried it with my consultancy business and it helped us capture and opt-in contact details for over 50,000 retailers (for a relatively small cost per lead).

Here's how it worked...

Scratchcard winners were sent to a capture page where they had to enter their winning code to discover their prize.

In terms of prizes, every scratchcard was a winner (to maximise the amount of opt-ins).

Prizes ranged from a relevant e-book to free meals, dessert, or wine (for restaurants) to Amazon vouchers and business books (for consulting practices) to racking and vouchers (for retailers).

Again, the scratchcard sat at the front end of the funnel. It was the conversation starter, which was followed up by emails, and in some cases telesales calls too.

The key with traffic generation is to take a passive AND an active approach – and experiment!

Growing your list organically through SEO, social media presence, and getting referrals works. But alongside this, you can accelerate the process by paying to get more eyes on your offer.

Remember, the prize here is a list of perfect customers that you can then contact.

When you OWN the list, you have a heap more control.

Cost-effective ways to drive traffic to your lead magnet

SOCIAL MEDIA

This is a really easy one. Simply post the URL of your capture page onto your social media timelines. Not only will this allow your lead magnet to be seen by a potential audience, but there's a high chance that your fans will share your offer – if it's compelling enough.

PAID TRAFFIC

Don't make the mistake of trying to build your list on the cheap. Instead, look at the potential return on any advertising budget that you spend to get people onto your list. Facebook ads work exceptionally well for lots of businesses. What's more, as Facebook is becoming more and more sophisticated, you're able to laser target your offer to the right target avatar.

BLOG POSTS

Write blog posts, which seamlessly lead into your lead magnet. The beauty of creating blog content is you're adding fresh content to your website – which could boost your chances of getting found in an organic search. In addition, a new blog is something else you can post onto social media – so it gives you a second bite of the cherry.

EMAIL

Remember to email your existing subscribers and let them know about your lead magnet – especially if they have yet to buy.

LEAFLETS

Consider running a leaflet drop that promotes your lead magnet and then drives people to your capture page to opt-in to get it.

A JOINT VENTURE

Your target customers are already buying from other, non-competing businesses. So do some research and see if you can build relationships with fellow business owners who are already talking to the people you want to attract. There may be some synergy whereby they can promote your lead magnet to their list – as long as there's something in it for them.

NETWORKING

With permission, you can add the contact details of people you've met at your networking events. It's a powerful way to continue the face-to-face conversation you started and ensure you stay in touch from meeting to meeting.

RETARGETING

Simply put a retargeting pixel on your website (your web technician can help) and you can start building a list of people who've looked at a specific page on your website but have not yet taken action. While you won't have email addresses, you can retarget visitors with adverts via Facebook and Google. You may have experienced this strategy for yourself. If a company has ever 'followed you' around the web, then you've been retargeted!

Step 4: Deliver your lead magnet and add opt-ins to your sales funnel

Once you've created your lead magnet and built your capture page, the next step is to integrate your **email marketing system**. There are two reasons for this:

1. To deliver your lead magnet

2. To gather and store the contact details you've collected into your sales funnel

As a general rule, the more information you request at the gateway to your lead magnet, the fewer subscribers you'll enlist. As an absolute minimum you want email addresses, but it may be worth asking for first names too so you can personalise your email communication, but again this is a variable you can test. Remember, telesales teams will need phone numbers, or enough information so they can search for the details online.

When it comes to email marketing systems, you have a huge range of options – and a full discussion of the pros and cons of each is far beyond the scope of this book. And remember, unless you're interested in web tech you don't need to know the intricacies of how the automation works. You just need to know the possibilities – so you can make the right decision for you and then find a web tech to help you implement everything (something we help clients with on a month-by-month basis).

To help kick-start your search, we recommend you take a look at **ActiveCampaign**. This is the email marketing system we use and the fuel that runs the keeping in touch element of all the done-for-you sales funnels we run for our clients. There is a link to this system in our Resources section, which we share with you at the end of the book. We also use Infusionsoft for more complex funnels.

ActiveCampaign is an easy-to-use sales and marketing system. It has a lot of functionality for a relatively small monthly investment. For example, with this tool you can:

- Send campaigns (one-off emails) as well as autoresponders

- Segment your list

- View results

- Create a pipeline of opportunities to aid follow-up

- And much, much more

One of the biggest benefits of email marketing software is it enables you to track and analyse your results. It means you're no longer operating in the dark, but can make an informed judgement on what works (and what doesn't).

Systems like these also beat using alternatives such as Outlook, which don't handle bulk, automated emails too well. MailChimp/Constant Contact and the like are good emailing systems, but lack the additional elements a full sales funnel needs.

Finally (and perhaps most significantly), once someone subscribes, those contact details are automatically added to your email list – and your database grows.

You don't have to manually do anything.

Your new contact gets what they signed up for and all is good. As a result, automating this part of your sales funnel can save you A LOT of time and money. That's because once it is set up it can just run and run and run.

WHICH SYSTEM WILL YOU USE?

Because there is so much choice it's always worth getting recommendations from other users – to help inform your choice. We can help you too. See the end of the book for information about how to arrange your free sales funnel consultation.

Step 5: Email onboarding and your first offer

So you've created a lead magnet, built a capture page, integrated your email marketing system, promoted your lead magnet, and got people into your list.

Great job!

But remember: you still need to make money!

So how do you convert the subscribers in your sales funnel into paying customers? Unless you can convert these leads, the money in your list remains pure potential.

And that's why what you do next is critical...

We recommend a simple **KLT, GLF sequence** – it's an asset that works for most businesses.

GLF, KLT is a **six-part email sequence** that aims to achieve the following:

- Build on the lead magnet in some way – so the sequence flows and feels seamless

- Build your authority by telling subscribers what you do

- Build rapport and connection by expressing your personality (or your business's) so that subscribers can get a good idea of what it would be like to work with you

- Proving you get real client results by sharing testimonials, case studies, or before and after images

- Making a one-off, low-price offer to subscribers – to encourage them to take the next step and become a customer (you'll be amazed how much stronger your relationship becomes when cash has exchanged hands)

- Following up and encouraging them to take the next step and work with you

The key with this process is to nurture your fledgling relationship.

You want to stimulate and continue conversations and make it easier for your subscriber to buy. It means when you make that all-important first offer, you've already done the groundwork – so it feels less annoying and pushy salesman-like!

Remember, your lead magnet is a crucial part of those foundations.

If you've chosen the right lead magnet, you've already given your prospect some value – upfront. What's more, if the lead magnet has enhanced their life in some way, then you've also transformed the way that you and your business are perceived. You're no longer seen as a pesky salesperson – but someone who's useful and helpful.

It means they'll be more likely to WANT to buy from you.

And it's a whole lot easier selling to someone who's warm than someone who is stone cold! But that's the principle of sales funnels... nudge (the right people) step-by-step through the process of becoming a customer. It feels a lot more comfortable from both the customer and the business perspective.

It's NOT your customer's job to remember to buy from you – it's YOUR job to stay in touch and give them a reason to buy... again and again.

And that's the power of the **KLT, GLF** sequence.

Here's an outline **(if you want to see one of ours then opt-in and follow the communication that comes out at www.salesfunnelsmadesimple.co.uk)**

KNOW	This email aims to build authority by showcasing our expertise and experience. In others words, this is about ensuring subscribers KNOW what you do – so that when they need your services they're clear that you can help.
	You could also see this email as a positioning piece designed to separate you from your competitors and put you in your category of ONE.
LIKE	When it comes down to business, people buy from people they like. The likeability factor is unpredictable because we all resonate with different people. So use this email to share some of your personality and aim to build that all-important rapport.

TRUST	This email is about proving you do what you say you do. There are many ways you could write this email. For example, you could include:
	• Before and after pictures
	• Written and video testimonials
	• Case studies
	The key here is the social proof.
	Remember, customers will always believe what others say about you far more than anything you could ever say yourself.
GAIN	Where the KLT sequence is about building relationships by allowing your subscribers to discover more about you, the GLF sequence is more concerned with encouraging them to take action.
	You can use this sequence to persuade customers to take the first step and buy a low-cost introductory offer, sign-up for a trial, or book a one-to-one (for example).
	The choice is yours – you simply need to figure out the next logical step in your sales funnel and focus this sequence on encouraging that.
	Your GAIN email should outline that offer (you may prefer to link to a dedicated sales page) and what the subscriber has to gain from taking you up on it. Remember to focus on benefits, not features. We buy based on what something can do for us, not because of its functionality.
	Remember to include a specific call to action – to increase the likelihood that your reader will respond.

LOGIC	While some people will respond to your GAIN email, not everyone will.
	Remember the principle of follow-up? Well it applies to this email sequence too. That's why your LOGIC email has the same objective as the GAIN email – but positions the offer in a slightly different way.
	In this email you want to appeal to someone's rational mind.
	What are the clear benefits to invest in your offer/What do they have to gain?
	Again, your call to action is key.
FEAR	If GAIN & LOGIC get no response, try the FEAR approach.
	Us humans are motivated by fear, which means if you focus on what your reader is risking or will lose out on by turning down your offer, you can get some great results.
	Your FEAR email can include some scarcity tactics (such as limited availability or time), but keep it real. Don't make stuff up to sell. Your clients will smell a rat!
	This is your last bite at the cherry.

But if readers don't respond, this isn't the end of the road. Remember, sales are often about timing. Your subscriber raised their hand when they opted-in for your lead magnet. They are interested in what you do; it's simply not the right time to buy.

That's why you need to keep in touch even after this initial onboarding sequence has finished. I'll explain how to do this in the next chapter.

THEORY INTO PRACTICE

To succeed with the KLT I GLF sequence you need to decide what you'll promote as the first step that you want customers to take – because this is what you'll promote during the sequence.

Here are some examples:

1. A free Site Survey to assess your business's specific security risk

2. A low price infoproduct

3. A free consultation (that adds value and helps to make a customer's buying decision easier)

Take some time now to brainstorm some possibilities for your business.

Summary

Sales funnels can be complex beasts – and for some businesses they need to be.

However, many businesses can get good results with a simple sales funnel – just like we've outlined above.

So don't let complexity put you off – especially now we've shown you where to start and what to implement. As a quick summary, here are the five assets you need to build the simple sales funnel we just outlined:

1. Create a **lead magnet**

2. Build an **opt-in page** (integrated into your website or in a standalone system such as Click Funnels, Lead Pages or Dan Harrison's SqueezePage Toolkit)

3. Connect up with your **sales funnel marketing system**

4. Decide how to **promote your lead magnet** so you can secure opt-ins

5. Follow-up and continue the conversation with the **KLT, GLF sequence**

With this simple system in place, you can attract more of the right people to your business without feeling like a pushy salesman.

It means every time someone new opts in to receive your lead magnet, they'll receive your give-to-get offer as well as your KLT, GLF sequence automatically – without you having to do a thing.

But that's not all. Your Getting Started funnel brings with it a whole range of other benefits too:

- Saves you time

- Boosts your productivity

- Increases efficiency

- Creates a standalone asset that works 24-hours a day

- Attracts more of the right leads

- Collects contact details – so you always have people

- Knows that you gave your subscriber real value

- Makes more sales through the rhythmic acquisition of customers

- Builds your profile

- Nurtures your know, like, trust factor

- Nurtures relationships

- Gets you out of the feast or famine trap

- Allows you to feel more in control

- Ensures everyone gets the same onboarding experience

- And more!

But what happens next? As you can imagine this isn't the end.

Firstly, you should revisit your lead magnet, opt-in page, and onboarding sequence periodically – to ensure it's still relevant and improve where appropriate. Check your metrics and analyse your numbers so you can test the performance of your sequence and identify what can be done to improve your results.

But that's not all...

By the end of your KLT I GLF sequence, a percentage of your leads will have converted and invested in the first step. A proportion of these customers will be interested in buying something else from you.

In comparison, others will remain prospects.

So what do you do next to maximise the return and longevity of your funnel?

That's what we're going to explore in chapter 4...

CHAPTER 4

HOW TO BUILD AND MAINTAIN MOMENTUM IN YOUR SALES FUNNEL

With your Getting Started funnel built and your first tranche of subscribers through, you'll have subscribers at different stages in your sales funnel.

1. Some will have invested in your getting started offer and will be so impressed they'll want to tell others

2. Some will have fallen in love with what you do and will want to buy more

3. Some haven't bought yet, but may well do if you ask them again or offer them something else

4. Finally, if you keep driving traffic to the top of your funnel, you'll have a series of new leads making their way through your funnel

Which means there's still work to be done if you want to get the best return from your investment.

So what should you do next?

The key is NURTURE. After all, it's not your customers' job to remember to do business with you… it's YOUR JOB to remind them.

And when it comes to making a purchase, I've said it already– it's all about the timing.

Last month may have been a 'no', but four weeks later and the situation within a business could have changed which means a no becomes a 'yes please!'

Consider this smart advice written by **Thomas Smith** way back in 1885. Yes, it may be 120 years old, but it's highly relevant now and sheds some light on why ongoing marketing is such a smart strategy to adopt:

1. **The first time people look at any ad they don't even see it**

2. **The second time, they don't notice it**

3. **The third time, they are aware that it is there**

4. The fourth time, they have a fleeting sense that they've seen it somewhere before

5. The fifth time, they actually read the ad

6. The sixth time, they thumb their nose at it

7. The seventh time, they start to get irritated by it

8. The eighth time, they start to think "here's that confounded ad again"

9. The ninth time, they start to wonder if they may be missing out on something

10. The tenth time, they ask their friends and neighbours if they have tried it

11. The eleventh time, they wonder how the company is paying for these ads

12. The twelfth time, they start to think that it must be a good product

13. The thirteenth time, they start to think the product has value

14. The fourteenth time, they start to remember wanting a product exactly like this for a long time

15. The fifteenth time, they start to yearn for it because they can't afford to buy it

16. The sixteenth time, they accept the fact that they will buy some in the future

17. The seventeenth time, they make a note to buy the product

18. The eighteenth time, they curse their poverty for not allowing them to buy this terrific product

19. The nineteenth time, they count their money carefully

20. The twentieth time, prospects see the ad, they buy what is offered

Now this doesn't mean it will take 20 touchpoints before someone buys from you, but it does make the point that regular marketing leaves less cash on the table than ad hoc, sporadic efforts.

To be clear, if you only create marketing when you need customers, you'll remain stuck in the feast and famine cycle, which is stressful, demotivating, and not good for business.

In other words, if your funnel ends at the KLT I GLF stage, you'll almost certainly be leaving cash on the table.

That's why the next step is to **identify further steps in your funnel** – so you can build on the momentum you've already created.

Specifically, what's the next logical action and touchpoint you can introduce to nudge people closer to a first or another sale?

For example, is it:

1. **Regular emails to your list** (complete with an offer/invitation) to ensure you stay on the radar and continue to build your 'know, like, trust' factor until the timing is right

2. If you have phone numbers is it **using telesales** to get on the phone with people and have a one-to-one chat

3. Or how about using **direct or lumpy mail** (because the letterbox is much less cluttered than the inbox) to move the conversation further

4. You could even use your sales funnel as a way to attract more warm leads by systematically asking new clients for **referrals** to other people who you could help

There are lots of options available to you – you simply need to figure out which is going to work for you.

So to help you decide, let's explore some of your options in more detail.

BUILDING MOMENTUM WITH EMAIL

Regardless of the strategies you try, we recommend that all businesses use email regularly.

After all, it's an easy, cheap, and quick way to reach lots of people.

Plus, with advanced email capability you're able to **segment your list** into different categories allowing you to send tailored messages to different groups of people – so you can generate the best return.

What's more, most email marketing systems enable you to **track the effectiveness** of your marketing. For example, you can see how many recipients have read your emails and opened your links to pages. It's all logged in the analytics giving you an in-depth insight into the performance of all your marketing campaigns.

Let me give you the low-down on an email strategy we implement for our clients.

The 52-week river

With your KLT I GLF sequence sent, your database of contacts will be used to receiving regular emails from you.

That's why this is a habit that you should continue.

We advocate emailing often – at a frequency that you feel you can stick with comfortably and consistently. This frequency could be:

- Daily (and if you think this sounds like overkill, there are many businesses that get great results with this)
- Weekly
- Fortnightly
- Monthly
- Or any combination in between

Emailing frequency is a hotly discussed topic, but as is often the case there is no one size fits all approach. Instead you need to experiment and explore to see what delivers the best results for you.

And if you're wondering what on earth you could write about so often, then we've got that covered for you too.

Content ideas do hold back a lot of businesses as does fear that you don't write well enough. But the truth is, once you allow your creative juices to flow you may find you have too many ideas to write about!

So to help unlock your creative juices, here's a list of ideas for your emails.

[And if you really don't want to do this yourself, you can always hire a copywriter to do it for you!]

1. Link out:

- Email a link to your latest blog post and entice existing subscribers back to your website
- Link to your social media platform – and continue the conversation elsewhere

- Share links to other useful content that will add value to your subscribers (or help you strengthen relationships with influencers and your contacts)

2. **Create story posts to share your ideas and experiences** (with a business message woven in):
   - What happened today? (Because inspiration for emails is all around)
   - Be controversial and challenge existing thinking or ideas
   - Be thought provoking
   - Share your breakthroughs, game-changers, and epiphany moments
   - Be inspiring or motivational
   - Share your ideas and methods
   - Record videos

3. **Educate by sharing your knowledge and expertise** (in your own unique way):
   - Checklists
   - How-tos
   - Cheat sheets
   - FAQ
   - Top tips

4. **Tell your clients' stories**
   - Before and after pictures
   - Case studies and success stories
   - Testimonials

5. **Promote**
   - Create an offer
   - Launch a new product
   - Upsell or cross-sell across your product range
   - Promote a JV (Joint Venture) offer
   - Promote a VIP or an early bird offer
   - Run a 'flash' sale

6. **Get a response**
   - Ask for feedback
   - Encourage your readers to share their experiences with you
   - Invite people to an event, webinar, etc.

7. **Leave your readers wanting more**
   - Create autoresponders and write a series
   - Open a loop and leave on a cliffhanger

As you can see, there's A LOT you can talk about.

THEORY INTO PRACTICE

Think you have nothing to email about?

If so, try this simple, creative exercise...

Set a timer for 15 minutes and write down as many topics or ideas you can think of in that time. Don't censor your ideas, just let them flow.

Then put to one side and come back and review at a later date. In amongst the weak ideas you will have some gems that will make excellent hooks, which you can use to converse with your list.

One-off campaigns and promotions

Your 52-week river isn't the only way to integrate email into the next stages of your sales funnel.

Your 52-week campaign can form the backbone of your follow-up operation. Once you've set your frequency and introduced the processes and checks to ensure those emails get written and scheduled, you'll have the peace of mind that your audience will continue to hear from you regularly.

But that doesn't mean these are the only emails you can send.

In addition, you can use the following:

- **One-off campaigns and promotions** – you can run flash sales, holiday offers, and other deals to encourage people to buy

- **Autoresponder campaigns** – create sequences to promote new offers and build interest and desire for products and services further up your Sales Ladder

- **Direct and lumpy mail** – because the letterbox is less competitive than the inbox

The point here is the more you're in contact, the stronger your relationships with your list and the more likely you are to persuade people to buy and climb further up your Sales Ladder.

Telesales

Another strategy that works brilliantly is telesales.

When I worked in the magazine business, we faced an interesting problem.

Most retailers didn't wake up thinking "the answer to my prayers is magazines!" Instead, we had to persuade them that mags could make a difference to their store.

At the time we supplied just a small percentage of the total retailer base, BUT we could get our hands on the contact data to market to the rest.

Now the same is probably true for your business.

It's likely you have a customer avatar and it's probable you can get hold of the data you need to start a conversation.

But what's the best way to market to a cold list?

With telesales we were able to add warm prospects to our funnel for as little as £1.50 a lead.

But here's the interesting thing...

Every person we add, we've spoken with PERSONALLY. Thanks to telesales, we've had a one-to-one call with every single lead that's opted into our list in this way.

All businesses understand the value of one-to-one calls, but most think telesales is far too expensive for lead generation. But if you think differently, it's surprising what different options you can create.

Enter the **Ghana Call Centre**. It's been helping get warm leads for us (and clients) for as little as £1.50 a lead. That's cheaper than the leads we can get through Facebook adverts for most sectors.

Many people don't realise that English is the Ghanaian official language. We pay an ethical wage, hand-pick staff (who have been screened for their language skills), and train them to have personalised conversations with prospects and clients.

And it works...

Telesales is far more personalised than email and other 'mass' communication strategies. This makes it more 'expensive', but the benefits can outweigh the cost. That's because you're able to understand and handle specific objections. You can also tailor the call to the needs and requirements of the person you are speaking with. In fact, we've found that telesales can skyrocket the return of a sales funnel by helping to close sales that otherwise would have been left dormant.

[If you'd like to discover more about the Ghana Call Centre and how you could use it in your business, visit www.salesfunnelsmadesimple.co.uk/ghana-call-centre.]

We also have a small team of Telemarketers based here in the UK for higher level sales and appointment getting. These help our Sales Funnels and Ghana Call Centre activity as well as doing some work for private clients. If this is of interest you can find out more by emailing tim@salesfunnelsmadesimple.co.uk with Telemarketing Enquiry in the headline.

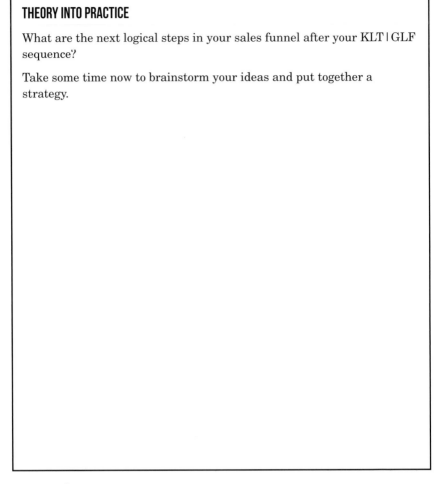

THEORY INTO PRACTICE

What are the next logical steps in your sales funnel after your KLT | GLF sequence?

Take some time now to brainstorm your ideas and put together a strategy.

Moving on...

The Getting Started funnel is just one funnel that you can implement in your business.

You may decide that the next step for you may be to build a second funnel to complement your existing funnel or to target a different client base altogether.

So if you're looking for some more advanced sales funnel strategies, we've got you covered in chapter 5.

CHAPTER 5
DIFFERENT TYPES OF SALES FUNNELS

A Getting Started funnel consisting of:

1. An opt-in page

2. Lead magnet

3. KLT | GLF sequence

Can be just the start point.

This sales funnel works really well for a whole range of businesses. It's a proven way to get started with using automation and content to attract your perfect customers and persuade them to take the first step.

But there's so much more you can do once you have the basics in place.

We're already spoke about the importance of follow-up and the role it has in nurturing relationships and making it more likely that people will buy.

- But what if you have a small, specific list of people you want to work with.

- What if you already have contact details?

- What if you want to invigorate lapsed customers?

- Or how about inviting existing customers to buy other products and services?

While the principles of nurture, follow-up, and close apply, sales funnels can be used flexibly across a whole range of business functions. For example, you can:

- Specifically target people you would LOVE to work with **(your 'dream' list)**

- Get old customers buying from you again **(lapsed customer funnel)**

- Persuade existing customers to buy other products and services **(upsell/cross-sell funnel)**

- Improve your ROI from speaking, networking, and exhibiting gigs **(face-to-face funnel)**

- Turn your latest book into a lead generator **(free + shipping funnel)**

Let's explore some of these in turn...

Dream List

We've built dream lists for a number of businesses and it's a strategy that works brilliantly.

The first time I used this strategy was in the magazine industry. While our Getting Started funnel had great success at securing lots of small retailers, we wanted to land a few of the bigger retail fishes. It was clear the starter funnel wasn't going to work for a business with gatekeepers and well protected buyers. Instead we needed to devise a new strategy that could cut through the layers of 'protection' and get us sufficiently noticed to land a face-to-face appointment with the retail buyers.

Enter the Dream List Funnel – something that also works brilliantly for helping consultants secure private clients.

Here's how you can use this funnel too.

WHAT IS A DREAM LIST?

A dream list is a hand-picked database of people you'd most like to work with.

As it's your dream list you can afford to be specific and even wishful. Include the people you think you have no hope of convincing – because if you get your campaign right then no one should be out of reach.

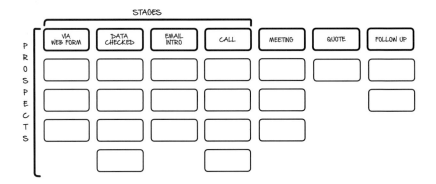

THEORY INTO PRACTICE

Most businesses only need a handful of new customers to completely transform their fortunes.

So rather than waiting for the right people to come to you, the Dream List funnel enables you to be proactive by creating a strategy that puts you in front of the people you'd most like to work with.

Here's how to build yours...

1. If you could wave a magic wand and secure any customer you like, who would make your dream list?

2. Brainstorm the touchpoints you need to create to start a conversation, build a relationship, and close the deal. (You'll find a real life example below.)

Dream List Case Study

A look over the shoulder

HOW WE CREATED A 21-STEP SALES FUNNEL TO DESIGNED TO SMASH PAST THE GATEKEEPER AND OVERCOME MAGAZINE MISCONCEPTIONS... JUST TO GET AN APPOINTMENT

The idea

It's not easy to get noticed by a retail buyer (or MD, or any other key person you want to connect with).

Retail buyers are always being pitched with the latest products or ideas and therefore they have to be ruthless with their time and attention. They're looking for every reason to say no, which makes their gatekeepers a tough bunch to crack!

So how do you cut through this?

First up you need to collect the names and contact details of the people you want to connect with. As your dream list is going to be relatively small you can afford to invest some manpower to get your hands on high-quality data and even check it. This part of the process could involve collecting data from LinkedIn or finding details on websites or other social media channels. You may even be able to get the information you need through other contacts.

The next step is figuring out how to make a statement so your message is noticed. For the magazine distributor, we decided to build a funnel based around 'lumpy mail' i.e. sending direct mail containing a physical 'grabber' in a round tube – rather than just an envelope. There are a few reasons for this:

1. **To get attention** – as more people rely on email, the letterbox has become less crowded making it easy to be noticed

2. **Curiosity** – with a physical item stuffed inside a tube, it's more likely to get opened as the recipient will want to know what it is... and being a tube it can't be put to the bottom of the pile!

3. **Memorable** – emails can quickly get forgotten and one click makes them disappear into the online abyss. A printed message is tangible and therefore has the stick around factor.

Once we'd decided to invest in lumpy mail we needed inspiration for what to send.

For inspiration, we brainstormed and also spoke to a range of promotional gift companies. We briefed them that we wanted new and different, not the usual array of pens and mugs. We also gave them an outline cost per item we had in mind too.

After creating a shortlist of products, we discussed some ideas to see how we could tie a message into the items we'd selected. After all, it's no point sending direct mail unless it ties into the message. Otherwise it will just appear random and confusing.

So for example:

- A light bulb could be linked to a bright idea
- A stringed tea bag can have a 'no strings attached' message
- Something gold can link to a golden opportunity
- A power bank can have the power of magazines, or recharge the outlet message

As you can see there's a ton of scope here to find a cost-effective grabber and then construct a sales message around it that's different and interesting.

THE FUNNEL

Due to the nature of the list we were targeting, it was unlikely a one-off letter would do the trick. Remember the principle of follow up? Persistence is key when you're attempting to break into a new retailer! As a result, we created a multi-step funnel that included:

1. **Direct mail** with as many as three separate lumpy 'grabber' letters if needed (we stop the campaign once we get an appointment)

2. **Follow-up messages** sent by email and LinkedIn… We use LinkedIn as well as email, as we find buyers manage their own LinkedIn accounts, but have assistants and gatekeepers to manage email

3. **Personalised video messages** sent via BombBomb – a video messaging tool we found

4. **An infographic** of the Magazine Myth Busters

5. **Follow-up** phone calls

6. **Topped off with a personalised video brochure**, with an infographic based video – again delivered in the post to create a powerful experience and grab their attention

And the purpose of this sales funnel?

To **sell a one-to-one appointment**. That's because we knew if we if he could get a face-to-face appointment with the buyer, it's possible to discuss the magazine opportunity tailored for the retail group.

THE SALES FUNNEL OVERVIEW

Goal of the campaign: To secure a 30-minute sales meeting with the retail buyer, in person.

Call to action: In every communication, the buyer is invited to book a face-to-face meeting to discuss the commercials of the magazine opportunity.

Phone calls: Follow up after every 'grabber' has been used.

STEP	AIM AND APPROACH	FORMAT
Pre-campaign	**Headline: Can you point me in the right direction please?** Email to a contact at the retail group to check we have the right contact details for the buyer.	Email & LinkedIn
1	**Headline: Here's a bright idea for your shops** Direct mail, which plays on the idea that magazines are a bright idea and then explains why.	Direct mail with light bulb grabber
2	**Headline: Did you hear that?** Short email acknowledging the fact that buyers are inundated with sales messages.	Email & LinkedIn
3	**Headline: Re: a bright idea** Email that refers to the bright idea letter and invites the buyer to book an appointment.	Email & LinkedIn
4	**Headline: Can I put a face to my name?** Contains a link to a video message so the buyer can see and hear from the person sending these messages.	Direct mail with link to personalised video
5	**PHONE CALL – focused on the bright idea**	

6	**Headline: False beliefs and wrong decisions** Email that calls out the magazine myths and tells them to keep an eye out for the printed infographic.	Email & LinkedIn
7	**Headline: Warning. You could be making a decision based on inaccurate information** Direct mail containing a printed infographic that exposes the myths about the magazine market and presents the truth.	Direct mail with printed infographic
8	**Headline: It's all lies!** Email to follow up receipt of the printed 'myth buster' infographic.	Email with infographic attachment
9	**PHONE CALL – focused on the myth busters**	
10	**Headline: Studies Reveal that 74% of The Population Read Print Magazines. So why not sell these bestselling niche and specialist titles in your shops?** Direct mail containing a bundle of magazines chosen for the retailers sector.	Direct mail with magazine bundle
11	**Headline: Which one was missing?** Email referring to the magazine bundle and asking the buyer if they'd like copies of any other titles.	Email & LinkedIn
12	**PHONE CALL – focused on the bundle**	
13	**Headline: Want more footfall? Then try this...** Email linking footfall to magazines and telling the buyer to be on the lookout for our book.	Email & LinkedIn
14	**Headline: Revealed. The simple secret to more footfall** Direct mail containing book about the link between footfall and magazines.	Direct mail with copy of Revealed book
15	**PHONE CALL – focused on the book**	
16	**Headline: *"So see every opportunity as golden, and keep your eyes on the prize - yours, not anybody else's."*** Direct mail containing a gold USB bar that explains 10 good reasons why magazines can become a gold mine for retailers.	Direct mail & gold USB stick

17	**Headline: 10 very good reasons** Email to follow the gold USB stick to reinforce the reasons why magazines are a golden opportunity.	Email & LinkedIn
18	**PHONE CALL – focused on the golden opportunity**	
19	**Video card** Highlighting the truth about magazines.	Video card
20	**PHONE CALL – focused on the video card**	
21	**Headline: Now, never, or later…** Email survey – asking the buyer when they want us to contact them.	Email & LinkedIn

One more thing…

The Dream List isn't only about finding customers.

You can use the same principles to help you find JV partners, strategic alliances, dream speaking/podcast gigs etc. The possibilities are endless.

LAPSED CUSTOMER FUNNEL

Here's a mantra for you. We have used it a number of times in the book and it's very important to remember…

> **It's not your customer's job to remember to buy from you. Instead, it's your job to remind them.**

The hardest transaction to secure is the first one. You need to get enough know, like, trust credits in the bank for the customer to feel comfortable enough to buy from you.

When money first exchanges hands, everything changes.

Customers have invested in you and your company. They are no longer just digesting free content and advice, they have decide to trust you to get them the results you promise.

And assuming you've delivered what you said you would, it should be a lot easier to persuade a lapsed customer to buy from you rather than always seeking out new people.

Remember, there are lots of reasons why people stop buying. For example:

1. Their circumstances may have changed

2. They may have forgotten you

3. You haven't asked them!

4. You neglected the relationship and now they are buying from someone else

5. They no longer need the product they used to buy from you and they don't realise you have other products that they now use instead

A **Lapsed Customer Funnel** works to reinvigorate this pool of potential by initiating a conversation and inviting them to take action. Aim to remind the customer that you were good together in the past and highlight all the things that you can do to make their life easier and better.

This funnel works best if you combine it with an offer. For example:

- A welcome back consultation - to discuss how you could help

- A welcome back coupon/discount/exclusive offer/voucher etc.

The key here is to give an incentive to encourage them to work with you again.

This funnel is super simple to set-up.

- First up decide who a lapsed customer is. This will vary depending on your sector. For example, it might be a few months for a restaurant, but 12 months for a cruise specialist.

- Then work your numbers to construct your offer.

- Craft a 2-3 part email sequence.

- Then when you've checked everything works, hit send!

Invest just a few hours of your time and you could freshen up some old relationships and add some additional sales to this month's total with a relatively small amount of effort.

And here's the thing…

Once written and tested, you can use this funnel again and again at appropriate times throughout the year.

UPSELL/CROSS-SELL FUNNEL

Fact, There may be as much as 30% growth locked up in your list – you simply have to identify it, nurture it, and release it.

And that's what the Upsell/Cross-Sell funnel is designed to do.

Let me explain...

You know your business inside out – and that's just the way it should be.

But here's the thing...

Just because you know your business intimately, doesn't mean your clients do. In fact, more often than not your prospects and customers will only know what you choose to tell them about your business.

This was certainly the case for a promotional goods business that we worked with.

While its core business was promotional merchandise, it also offered a collection of other relevant products and services including exhibition stands and embroidered workwear.

As you'd expect, these three products had three different target avatars.

What's more, even if a single business wanted all three services, it wasn't unusual for different decision-makers to be in charge of each.

As a result, this promotional goods company was sitting on a pile of unexplored business – simply because it hadn't told its customers the other products and services on offer.

The Upsell/Cross-Sell Funnel solves this. If you undertake activity that enables you to grow each of the variables by 10%, you achieve 33% growth.

Here's a matrix that can help...

Clients	Frequency	Value	Turnover
100	2	£1,000	£200k
110	2	£1,000	£220k
110	2.2	£1,110	£262.2k

33% + Growth

And a super easy way is to bolt an email campaign onto the end of your KLT\GLF sequence.

In addition, you can include reminders and pitches in your 52-week river.

One more thing…

Where different people are responsible for buying different products, ask your contact to connect you with the person/people you need to speak with. You can automate this request by:

- Including an email as part of your funnel
- Including a reminder in your workflow to ask a customer if they'd be interested in the other things you sell at a relevant point in your relationship

Try it for yourself and see.

FACE-TO-FACE FUNNEL

Speaking, exhibiting, and networking are all brilliant ways to build your profile and make new connections.

But are you capitalising on the leads you secure or letting them go to waste?

If you're not proactively following-up with the people who have heard you speak, then you are leaving sales on the table. Fortunately there's an easy way to keep the conversation going after the event/meet-up has finished.

Enter your Face-to-Face funnel.

If you're a speaker, ensure you include a **How To Get More** slide at the end of your presentation.

Use this slide to take people to a capture page where they can enter their details to get copies of your slides as well as any other goodies and freebies you want to throw into the mix.

From an audience perspective, this is a positive approach. How many times have you missed a key part of a presentation because you were frantically trying to copy a slide or take a photo. This strategy avoids the need for that…

… AND ensures you leave with the contact details of the people who were in the audience.

In turn, you can kick-start a KLT or sales sequence designed to turn a cold audience into a warm list of leads and raving customers.

You can also do something similar to capitalise on leads from exhibitions and networking.

For example, if you're exhibiting use your marketing bumf to send people to a capture page where they can sign-up to get more stuff. Similarly, add a URL to your business card that directs new contacts to a page that's going to kick-start a funnel designed to nurture new leads and build that all-important know, like, trust factor.

This simple tweak to your 'out and about' strategy could make the difference between time wasted and the sales pumping.

FREE + POSTAGE

There are a few ways you may have got yourself a copy of this book:

1. You got it at an event

2. You bought it on Amazon

3. You got it free when you paid for postage

If it was the third option, then you've already experienced - first-hand - the *free + postage funnel*.

Either way, let me explain how it works...

As you know, content sells. It's a powerful way to position yourself as the expert and build your *know, like, trust factor*.

But with masses of content being published each day, you have to think smart about how you'll stand out, differentiate yourself, and attract the attention of your perfect customer.

A book is a proven and powerful way to do that. What's more, with the explosion of self-publishing it's easier than ever to create a book with your name on it. You no longer have to secure an agent and with print on demand and batch printing options, you don't have to invest a small fortune getting your expertise into the pages of a book.

Instead you can beat the competition by sharing valuable information that boosts your positioning at the same time.

Free + postage is where you offer something for free, but (as the name suggests) charge for the postage and handling. That way you can cover some (even all) of the costs of the offer while still giving your customers a great deal.

This funnel has been tried and tested by experts and their books, but you can also use it for physical products too. For example, a survival ecommerce store offers a free credit card penknife at the front end of their funnel. Many in the USA offer free T-shirts or caps. You simply need to cover the postage and it's yours.

This funnel has a number of big benefits:

- Any leads will already have paid something. It may only be to cover the postage, but these leads are likely to be higher quality than the freebie hunters who aren't even willing to pay a few pounds to cover some stamps!

- Because your lead generation is partly funded, you can afford to spend more on your customer acquisition strategy by offering something more valuable at the front-end of the funnel

- You can offer something of higher value without increasing your costs

Here's what this funnel looks like in practice.

THEORY INTO PRACTICE

In addition to your Getting Started funnel, what other funnels could your business benefit from?

1. Explore the pros and cons for each of the five options below:

- Dream list
- Lapsed customers
- Upsell/cross-sell
- Face-to-face
- Free + Postage

2. Make a plan – what funnel will you focus your attention on next?

Moving on...

To date, we've given you A LOT of information to help you embed sales funnels into your business.

If you're still not convinced about the power of a sales funnel, read on with chapter 6 – this contains a sales funnel mythbuster and it exposes myths that prevent businesses getting started in the first place. Alternatively, turn to chapter 7 where we get under the surface of some of the challenges that businesses encounter when building a funnel and show you how to fix them.

CHAPTER 6
SALES FUNNEL MYTH BUSTER

Despite the huge range of benefits, many businesses have yet to build their own sales funnel.

We've found it's often down to one of these popular 'myths'.

MYTH 1. A SALES FUNNEL WON'T WORK FOR MY BUSINESS

It can be a costly mistake to dismiss a tactic because you believe your business is different and therefore what has worked elsewhere won't work for you.

So stay open-minded…

Remember, when it comes to sales funnels it isn't a one-size-fits-all solution. Instead, you can tailor your funnel so it best suits your business, your clients, and your objectives:

Sales funnels DO work in all types of business – whether that's B2B, B2C, online and off or whether you're attracting clients, customers, or patients. We've built (and managed) sales funnels for a whole range of businesses including printers, commercial cleaners, alarm installers, business consultants, and window and door resellers.

Regardless of what you are selling, the principles remain the same.

Once you've identified the key stages (as outlined above), you can experiment with different steps. Split test, remove redundant steps, and scale what works to boost your ROI. Your sales funnel is not set in stone.

MYTH 2. I TRIED USING A SALES FUNNEL BEFORE – IT DIDN'T WORK FOR ME THEN AND IT WON'T WORK FOR ME NOW.

Many businesses fail to get the desired results because they collect the wrong leads, or give up on a prospect too soon. Did you know that most sales are made after at least eight touchpoints? But despite this, many businesses give up after two or three points of contact.

If you do, then you're almost certainly leaving money on the table.

With a sales funnel, you can:

- Automate follow-up

- Distribute content

- Segment leads – helping you pinpoint the hottest enquiries and then use your sales team wisely

In other words, use the ideas and strategies outlined in this book and there's a good chance that you could introduce a simple sales funnel into your business that will deliver worthwhile results.

MYTH 3. I'VE GOT ENOUGH CUSTOMERS NOW SO I DON'T NEED A SALES FUNNEL.

Many businesses get caught in the 'feast or famine syndrome'. They're overrun with customers one month, then struggle to find sales the next.

A sales funnel is even more important if you currently enjoy peaks and troughs in your trade. By investing in the rhythmic acquisition of more leads and customers, you can create a more consistent, predictable business.

Here's how a sales funnel can give you peace of mind:

- It future-proofs your business by ensuring you have a constant stream of fresh leads entering the top of your funnel

- It helps you take a proactive (not reactive) approach to business so it becomes more sustainable and predictable

- It uses content to nurture leads and build relationships consistently – so you can close more sales and boost your company's performance

MYTH 4. I DON'T HAVE THE TIME TO SET UP A SALES FUNNEL.

As with anything new, it can take time to implement and set up your sales funnel, but the time you invest now will likely save you a disproportionate amount of time in the future.

Here's how:

- A sales funnel will eliminate unnecessary, costly repetition from your business

- You'll know exactly what's necessary to move a prospect through your funnel – so no more guesswork or making it up as you go along

- A sales funnel will help you quickly qualify the hottest leads so you waste less time on prospects that are not a good fit for you and your business

- As it's automated, your sales process can work 24/7 – you don't have to be in the office to reap the benefits

- What's more, you don't have to do this work yourself. This is a task that can be easily outsourced to an expert.

MYTH 5. SALES FUNNELS ARE TOO COMPLICATED.

It's tempting to dismiss a good idea because you don't understand it. Sales funnels rely on tech, processes, and content creation. If these skills are out of your comfort zone, you can feel daunted. But you needn't be:

- A car is complicated under the bonnet. That's why people rely on the dashboard to know what's working (and what isn't). It's the same with a sales funnel… you don't need to know the mechanics, just the metrics.

- Most small businesses can reap huge benefits from a relatively simple sales funnel (we showed you exactly how to build this in chapter 2.)

MYTH 6. SALES FUNNELS ARE TOO EXPENSIVE.

Whilst a sales funnel will incur some upfront costs, once implemented you can look forward to more sales and ultimately more profits. Here's why:

- You're likely to convert more leads into customers as the necessary touchpoints are identified and therefore not missed.

- You can automate some of the stages, which means you don't need a member of staff to do that work (and can therefore close more deals for less).

- A sales funnel can eliminate costly repetition and increase the efficiency of your sales process.

- Automation can free up you and your staff to focus on other business building and profit generating activities.

- Once set up, your sales funnel can provide tracking and conversion data so you know what sections are working and what aren't. As a result, you get access to the information and insights that help you to iron out niggles and glitches and ultimately increase your conversion rate.

- Automated follow-up at predetermined times can prevent fewer leads leaking through the gaps and therefore boosting your sales conversion – leaving less money on the table.

In short, there are numerous ways that a sales funnel will not only pay for itself, but boost your company's revenues and profits too. Once your sales funnel is working, investment at the top of the funnel will result in greater returns at the other end.

MYTH 7. A SALES FUNNEL IS TOO IMPERSONAL AND LACKS THE HUMAN TOUCH.

Business is all about people, so you may be worried about 'forcing' prospects into a predetermined funnel. But as you'll see, a process can add professionalism to your business, which many of your clients will appreciate.

Here's how:

- First impressions matter, so get it right by defining your sales funnel and ensuring all leads receive the same experience.

- A sales funnel allows you to formalise the stages that leads move through on their journey to becoming your customer. By mapping out the interactions you need (and don't need) you can boost efficiency and give prospects a more professional experience of your business.

- A documented sales funnel brings consistency to your client interaction. It ensures every lead receives the same information at the same point in the process – therefore delivering a similar experience for every new contact.

- You can add in whatever touchpoints are relevant and appropriate for your business. In short, you can support automated email with phone calls or meetings at the relevant stages of the sales cycle or weave in direct and lumpy mail too.

- Many businesses fail to follow-up and stay in touch. In short, an automated touchpoint is better than no touchpoint at all.

- Automated content needn't feel impersonal. If you write conversationally and to one person – even when creating a broadcast campaign, the recipient can still read your communication as if it was personalised to them.

- When you introduce automation into your sales funnel, you free up your sales team to have more time to invest on closure conversations.

The strategy set out in the design of your sales funnel is fundamental and it is a starting point we always use with clients through all our coaching and advisory services.

MYTH 8. A SALES FUNNEL WILL BE TOO DIFFICULT TO MANAGE.

- Once you've mapped out your process, you'll be managing a system instead of being held back by a haphazard, ad hoc approach.

- Once the system is in place, you'll have the peace of mind that it's working hard for you 24/7.

- A sales funnel can support your sales team and make them more efficient and effective. With a process to manage, it's easier to set goals and targets.

DOWNLOAD OUR MYTHBUSTER AT WWW.SALESFUNNELSMADESIMPLE.CO.UK

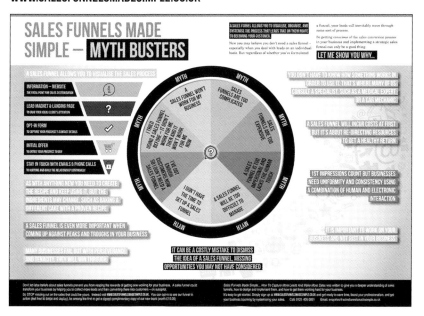

CHAPTER 7

SALES FUNNEL TROUBLESHOOTING

7 sales funnel mistakes and how to overcome them

Despite the relative ease of building a sales funnel, not all businesses get the results they need or expect.

Why is that?

Let's explore some of the most common sales funnel mistakes – and how you can avoid them.

This handy resource is an asset you can return to again and again as you get stuck into the business of funnels.

MISTAKE 1. YOUR OFFER ISN'T CONVERTING

If this is the case, you need to go revisit your funnel and take a decision as to what else you could offer to convert prospects into customers.

To help, here are some tips on crafting an offer that can ignite your sales funnel.

Offers form a key part of your sales funnel because an offer can help overcome buyer inertia and encourage prospects to BUY NOW. In addition, offers can:

1. **The right offer can help you overcome poor copy.** That's right! If you have a truly awesome offer, even if you don't write about it in the right way, you can still get a great result. In comparison, even the best copywriter in the world will struggle to sell an offer that frankly sucks.

2. **Helps overcome buyer inertia.** It's really difficult to convince people to reach for their wallet – particularly if this is their first transaction with you. A cracking offer can help lower the guard and convince customers that it's time to invest. And once a customer has bought once (assuming you handled the transaction properly), there's a very good chance they'll buy again.

3. **Overcome buyer's remorse.** Buying is a pleasurable experience (it's why some people get addicted). Endorphins and other feel good hormones are released when a customer makes up their mind to buy. But after the high, comes buyer's remorse. The peak feeling has disappeared leaving your customer wondering if they made a mistake. Regret sinks in... unless your offer blew them away! A really good offer can help sustain that retail high, and that's a good thing, don't you agree?

4. **Market research.** That's right, the performance of an offer is a blinding way to discover more about your customer's motivations and buying habits. So test. Experiment. See which price points and offer packages convert the best and use those insights to ensure your future marketing efforts grow your retail profits.

5. **Create a buzz!** As you know, the experience that customers have when shopping with you is incredibly influential. And the right promotion is just brilliant at creating a buzz and buoyancy – that can spread via word of mouth on social media.

6. **Grow your community of paying customers.** We've already mentioned how the first transaction is often the most challenging, but it also represents the biggest relationship shift. There's a big difference between a browser/prospect and a paying customer. If you can convince a shopper to part with their money once, it's far easier to do it again and again and again.

OK, so now that you understand the key reasons for including an offer as part of your sales funnel, let's explore what makes a cracking offer...

REVEALED!
THE ANATOMY OF A COMPELLING OFFER

Now you may be tempted to offer a big discount as your convert offer, but you don't need to.

Price is never a good differentiator on which to compete. Someone can ALWAYS undercut you, which means you'll quickly find yourself in a depressing "race to the bottom".

It's true that price discounts can work, but it's worth exploring other strategies to create compelling offers without killing your markup.

Here are a few examples to try in your sales funnel:

1. **Discounts** – can work, but treat these with caution. You absolutely MUST know your numbers and give some serious thought to the back-end. For starters, avoid the vanilla, predictable, boring 10% discount. This really won't entice people to buy and slices your profits significantly (as we've already seen). In addition, think through your strategy. If you're prepared to take a "hit" because you have something to upsell in the back-end, offering a deeper discount could be a smart approach.

2. **Free gifts** – consider offering a free complementary product. This can work particularly well if the freebie encourages the customer to buy that product in the future.

3. **Free information** – place a monetary value on e-books and other paper-based extras and include these as a bonus.

4. **Free face-to-face time** – this can work well in niche shops where your specialist knowledge is of value. For example, you could offer free workshops or "ask the expert" sessions or a VIP event for your best customers (or the prospects you want to convert into high value customers). Not only will this change the dynamics of your offer, but you can encourage people to use more products as well as build loyalty.

5. **Staged payments** – if a customer is making a sizeable investment, you may want to break up payments into more easily digestible chunks. Again, you'll need to think this through and ensure you have robust terms in place. This may not be suitable, but it could work in some places.

6. **Packages** – lump together a selection of products and services to upsell along with the core product purchase. Remember, it's better for you to add value than to lose margin by discounting.

When it comes to presenting and positioning your offer, they these:

- **Non-moveable deadline:** Frame the offer to persuade people to buy within a fixed timeframe (don't try and be "generous" and let the deadline slip. Do this and you'll annoy people who did buy before cut off, as well as setting an understanding that your deadlines are up for negotiation).

- **Urgency:** Get people revved up to buy now, with limited availability, limited time offers etc. If people believe that they are going to miss out, they can be persuaded to buy.

- **Genuinely discounted:** BOGOFs, a two for one deal, half-price sales, and other deep discounts can be very attractive. After all, we all love to get a bargain, don't we? However, don't artificially double your price and then reduce it. Do that and you'll undermine your integrity. In addition, make sure you've done your numbers here. A price-led strategy must generate profits somewhere, or your business can't survive long-term.

- **Crazy prices:** When you have a clear back-end in place and you know that one sale will lead to many more, you may wish to offer a specific product at a crazy price. A really good example of this is a high-end guitar seller based in the States. He knows his ideal customers use A LOT of plectrums. As a result, he sells plectrums at a crazy price on eBay. Now, he doesn't make any money on the plectrums. In fact, he probably just covers his costs. But that's OK. He's not looking to make money on plectrum sales. Instead, he's looking to build his list of customers who may wish to buy a high-end guitar in the future. As a result, his back-end is to stay in touch with the customers who buy plectrums, and he creates marketing to promote guitars.

Could you do something similar to this in your business?

- **Loss leaders:** There may be times that you sell a product at a loss. A loss leader may be a great way to boost footfall and get people into your shop. But again, you need to think through the back-end. Loss leaders only work if you can recoup your loss elsewhere – and that's why it all comes back to the numbers again. There's one more thing you can do to make your offer more believable and more compelling.

Simply give customers a REASON as to why you're offering a promotion.

Here's how it works...

Customers like to be able to rationalise a purchase – even if it's at a subconscious level. So if you're offering a really awesome, "too good to be true" deal, you need to explain why. If you don't, less people will buy because the cynicism will set in and put people off. Seriously!

So for example, if you are offering a valuable free gift with a purchase, you could explain that you're overstocked, that's it's your birthday, or whatever. Find a reason and make it genuine... and then your most compelling offers will sell even better. (We'll give you some more reasons to run offers shortly).

What other offers could you weave into your sales funnel to secure that first sale and nudge customers along your Sales Ladder?

MISTAKE 2. TRYING TO DO IT ALL YOURSELF

There are a number of skills that go into building a simple sales funnel that works. You need:

- **STRATEGY and VISION**. You need to map out your sales ladder, figure out your objectives, identify the pitfalls and barriers, and understand what you want your leads to do now, next, and later. Get the strategy wrong, and your funnel will disappoint. In comparison, hone down the big picture and you'll ensure all the other pieces fall into place easily.

- **CONTENT & COPY**. Content drives and fuels your sales funnel so you're going to need to put on your copywriting hat to craft persuasive words that build your *know, like, trust* factor. From crafting emails to picking ideas for blogs and lead magnets, the quality at all stages of your sales funnel is going to influence your results.

- **WEB TECH & DESIGN**. From building capture pages to setting up autoresponders and segmenting your list, it's key you set-up your back end to work smoothly so that you get the most from the benefits of automation.

- **DESIGN**. With so much content being thrust under the gaze of your target customer, it's key your brand and designs stand out and grab attention.

- **PAY PER CLICK**. It is possible to find customers through organic traffic alone, but if you want to accelerate your results you'll want to invest in paid advertising - whether that's on Google or social media.

- **SALES**. From structuring kick-ass offers to getting on the phone and closing the deals, you need to wield your powers of persuasion to convince customers that you are the perfect choice for them.

It's possible to do all these roles yourself, however this can lead to overwhelm, which can slow you down and put up unnecessarily roadblocks. So rather than struggling to do it all yourself, think back to your lifetime customer value and work out how much you can invest to get the help you need.

If you want to do it yourself, find people who can do the jobs that you can't. You can do this by:

- Employing staff so you have the in-house resource to fill all these roles

- Finding contractors or freelancers with the specific skills needed to manage and build the various parts of your funnel

- Outsourcing to experts in the UK or overseas

Alternatively, we can build your sales funnel for you (and take care of all the jobs listed above) from as little as £250 a month.

To have an initial chat just call us on 0121 405 0919 or email Tim@salesfunnelsmadesimple.co.uk. Tim, who heads up our sales and account management team, will be happy to chat about options for you.

MISTAKE 3. PITCHING TOO SOON

Sales is all about timing.

You may hit it at the perfect moment where the wallet is out. Other times you may be nurturing and building a relationship for many months before the customer is ready to say 'go'.

The key is to ensure you put value in the relationship up front.

It's a little like a bank account. You have to put in the credits first before you can make a 'withdrawal' by asking for a sale. If you make too many debits, you'll go into 'overdraft' - and that doesn't make for a profitable relationship. To put it another way, make sure you've done enough 'wooing' before asking a prospect to buy. Pitch too early (with the wrong offer) and you could turn people off before the relationship has even had a chance to get out of the starting blocks!

MISTAKE 4. NOT PITCHING AT ALL!

It's not uncommon for business owners to avoid asking for the sale - for lots of reasons. For example:

- They feel uncomfortable

- They don't know how to ask

- They 'forget'

The easiest way to overcome this is to weave an offer into your KLT, GLF sequence.

- Then get into the habit of making a regular pitch in your 52-week river. You can do this in a number of ways:

- Make the email about the pitch

- Include a pitch as a P.S.

- Send readers to a landing page with an offer or a blog post with a more subtle sale woven in

Remember, it's not your customer's job to remember to do business with you. It's your job to ASK them. What's more, you've got to ask regularly. And if you do feel uncomfortable, don't forget that your paid-for services are where your clients are going to get the biggest results.

MISTAKE 5. NOT UNDERSTANDING YOUR CUSTOMERS/AUDIENCE

Lots of businesses make the mistake of building their sales funnel with content that simply does not appeal to their target customer.

If you want people to engage with and respond to your content and your offers, they have to feel relevant to the people you want to attract. This means they need to:

- Enter the conversations that are happening inside your perfect customer's head

- Offer the solutions and answers your clients want

- Solve the challenges your clients are experiencing

- Use language, concepts, and ideas that your perfect customer resonates with

- Talks to the person receiving the information as an individual - not a generic group

- Acknowledges who they are and the sort of life they lead (and the dreams they have)

If you're not seen as relevant, you WILL get ignored and overlooked. That's why your customer avatar is such important and necessary preparation work.

MISTAKE 6. FAILING TO AUTOMATE

The BIG benefits of a sales funnel come from the autopilot elements.

When you remove unnecessary repetition and set things up to go out automatically, it removes items from your to-do list and frees up brain space for you to focus on other things.

If you try to do everything yourself, you'll miss emails, forget to follow-up and get yourself in a tangle. This is a total waste of your time and a drain on your energy. Instead, ensure you understand fully the capability of your chosen automation software (so you can make best use of all the features). Alternatively, find yourself a web tech expert you trust who can advise and do some of the implementation work for you so that you can get the best results possible.

MISTAKE 7. NOT KEEPING IN TOUCH

Sales funnels are built on consistency and persistency.

You've got to keep the content and communication flowing to maximise your results. Remember, you'll need more than a couple touchpoints to close a sale. You've got to be in it for the long-haul and that means consistent and persistent communication.

The key message here is DON'T GIVE UP TOO SOON, and pardon our language... BUT

DON'T F@*K UP THE FOLLOW-UP!

And on a similar vein, avoid the communication blast followed by radio silence. Consistency will get you much better results than sporadic activity. What's more, once you get yourself into the routine of regular communication and follow-up, you're more likely to make it a habit and keep going.

THEORY INTO PRACTICE

What pitfalls will you encounter as you build your sales funnel?

Make a note of your challenges below and take some time to get clear on how you'll overcome them.

SALES FUNNELS
MADE SIMPLE

IF YOU NEED HELP IMPLEMENTING YOUR OWN SALES FUNNEL, CALL THE EXPERTS!

The Sales Funnels Made Simple team are here to help you get more customers.

Sign up at www.salesfunnelsmadesimple.co.uk or contact us on the number below and let's get your business booming by systemising your sales!

 0121 405 0919

 tim@salesfunnelsmadesimple.co.uk

WWW.SALESFUNNELSMADESIMPLE.CO.UK

CHAPTER 8
YOUR NEXT STEPS

If you want to capture more leads and make more sales while reducing the overwhelm and clawing back time, you need to invest in a sales funnel.

A sales funnel is going to help reduce the feast or famine syndrome that slips a lot of businesses up and help you achieve the rhythmic acquisition of customers.

Once in place, you can set a chunk of your sales and marketing activity to run on autopilot and you'll also lay strong foundations, which will help you grow and scale your business.

If you're new to sales funnels, it can feel overwhelming. After all, there is a fair amount to do to get your first starter funnel set up.

You've got to do your preparation – this involves identifying your target customer and knowing your numbers.

Then you need to map out the various stages of your funnel:

- What will you use as a lead magnet?
- What email software will you use?
- What starter offer will you make?
- What will you include in your KLT | GLF sequence?
- How are you going to follow-up? For example, will you use telesales or add in some direct mail?
- And what will you do once the starter funnel is set up to build profitable relationships and ensure you leverage the full range of opportunities that exist in your list?

And if you do already have a funnel in place, how can you be sure it's set up optimally?

Hopefully, this book has given you some strong foundations for you to work on.

But this is just the start. That's one of the things that makes a sales funnel so powerful. You can build on it and expand it out – for the benefit of your business.

When it comes to sales funnels, we're here to make them simple.

Together with my team of hand-picked experts, we're here to help you get a sales funnel that works, delivers results, and helps you achieve your business goals.

So if you'd like our help, here's what to do.

1. **Firstly, opt-in at www.salesfunnelsmadesimple.co.uk**. This will get you on our list (so you can see a KLT, GLF sequence in practice). You'll also be able to get your hands on some funnel diagrams so you can have a think about what your business needs.

2. **Book your free sales funnel consultation with one of our experts**. If you're keen to get started, but want help to do so, our sales funnel experts are on hand to help. Whether you want an existing funnel critique, or some ideas and advice to help you create the funnel your business needs, your first hour is on us. To book your call, visit www.salesfunnelsmadesimple.co.uk.

3. **Take action!** Strategy and ideas are one thing, but nothing happens until you take action. So whether that's working out an action plan to implement yourself or investing in the support and expertise needed to get it done for you, do something! Remember, we have a team of experts on hand and ready to design, build, and maintain the sales funnel your business needs. Covering everything from strategy to copy to web tech and implementation, we can help you get the funnel you need with minimal input and effort from you.

4. **Get access to links and bonus resources** mentioned in the book at **www.salesfunnelsmadesimple.co.uk/book-resources**

5. And if the time's not quite right for you, but you'd like some guidance, mentoring and accountability added to your sales process then join one of my other services such as:

   • Business Alchemist (**www.business-alchemist.co.uk**)

   • Or see if my higher level Non Exec Director service is maybe more suitable (**www.barry-allaway.com/non-exec-director**)

Remember, we're only a phone call or email away so don't struggle alone. Instead, reach out and let us help you get results.

For more details, visit www.salesfunnelsmadesimple.co.uk

SALES FUNNELS
MADE SIMPLE

BOOK
RESOURCES

GET ACCESS TO THE RESOURCES
MENTIONED IN THIS BOOK HERE:

WWW.SALESFUNNELSMADESIMPLE.CO.UK/BOOK-RESOURCES

111

ARE YOU MISSING OUT ON SALES OPPORTUNITIES BECAUSE YOU JUST DON'T HAVE THE TIME?

ARE YOU NOT ACQUIRING ENOUGH WARM LEADS, SO YOUR BUSINESS GROWTH IS SLOWING DOWN?

WOULD HAVING A TELESALES TEAM MAKE YOUR BUSINESS RUN A LOT SMOOTHER?

Call Tim Cooper-Cocks on
0121 405 0919

Quote: "Sales Funnels Made Simple Book"
and get 10 days of calls for £600.

*That's a saving of £200 on our day rate and
£175 on-boarding fee*

WWW.SALESFUNNELSMADESIMPLE.CO.UK/GHANA-CALL-CENTRE